W0320795

zusammengestellt von Dietrich Kessler

KDM
VERLAG

29,80

Alle Rechte vorbehalten
© 1992 Copyright by KDM Verlag, Schwerinstraße 5, 1000 Berlin 30
Tel.: (0 30) 2 16 34 97, Fax: (0 30) 2 16 33 24
Gestaltung: Nele Ellerich
Repro: Schulz & Schulz GmbH, Berlin
Druck: Kupijai & Prochnow, Berlin
Printed in Germany
ISBN 3-927503-09-6
Bestell-Nr. 20984-23

Interpreten

AHA
Louis Armstrong
Animals
Joan Baez
Beach Boys
Beatles
Bee Gees
Harry Belafonte
The Byrds
Boney M.
David Bowie
Laura Branigan
Big Bill Broonzy
Eric Burdon
CCR
Roger Chapman
Eric Clapton
Joe Cocker
Judi Collins
Phil Collins
Bing Crosby
Miles Davis
Deep Purple
Depeche Mode
Doors
Bob Dylan
Jose Féliciano
Foreigner
Nina Hagen
Bill Haley
David Hasselhoff
Jimi Hendrix
The Hollies
Johnny and the Hurricans
Mahalia Jackson
Jethro Tull
Elton John
Janis Joplin
Jon Bon Jovi
Udo Jürgens
Ben E. King
Kingston Trio
Alexis Korner
Cindy Lauper
Led Zeppelin
John Lennon
Les Humphries Singers
The Lords
Madonna
Manfred Mann's Earthband
Bob Marley
Ricky Nelson
Mike Oldfield
Carl Lee Perkins
Plastic Ono Band
Police
Elvis Presley
Prince
Procol Harum
Queen
Lou Reed
Little Richard
Rolling Stones
Sandra
Sandpipers
Pete Seeger
Tony Sheridan
Frank Sinatra
Jimmy Somerville
Spencer Davis Group
Steppenwolf
Rod Stewart
Scorpions
Sting
Supertramp
Tears for Fears
Umberto Tozzi
Tina Turner
Uriah Heep
Wishful Thinking
Stevie Wonder
Zucchero / Paul Young

Inhalt

AS TEARS GO BY

Musik und Text:
Keith Richards/ Mick Jagger
Interpreten: Rolling Stones
Rhythmus: Rock Ballade
Tempo: Slow

© 1964 by Essex Music Ltd.
Für D, A, CH:
Nero Musikverlag Gerhard Hämmerling oHG

2. My richness can't buy everything
I want to hear the children sing
All I hear is the sound
of rain falling on the ground
I sit and watch as tears go by.

3. It is the evening of the day
I sit and watch the children play
Doing things I used to do
Thinking of you
I sit and watch as tears go by.

Auld lang syne

Traditional
Interpret: Joan Baez
Rhythmus: Ballade
Tempo: Moderato

2. We twa ha'e ran about the braes
And pu'd the gowans fine,
We've wandered many a weary foot
Sin auld lang syne.

3. We twa ha'e sported i' the burn
Frae mornin' sun till dine,
But seas between us braid ha'e roared
Sin auld lang syne.

4. And here's a hand my trusty friend,
And gie's a hand o' thine.
We'll take a cup of kindness yet
For auld lang syne.

A WHITER SHADE OF PALE

Musik und Text:
Keith Reid / Gary Brooker
Interpreten: Procol Harum
Rhythmus: Rock Ballade
Tempo: Moderato

© by Westminster Music Ltd.
Für D, A, CH: Essex Musikvertrieb GmbH, Köln

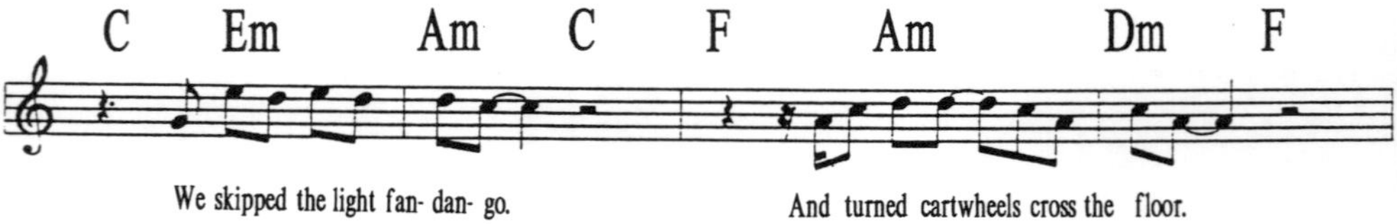

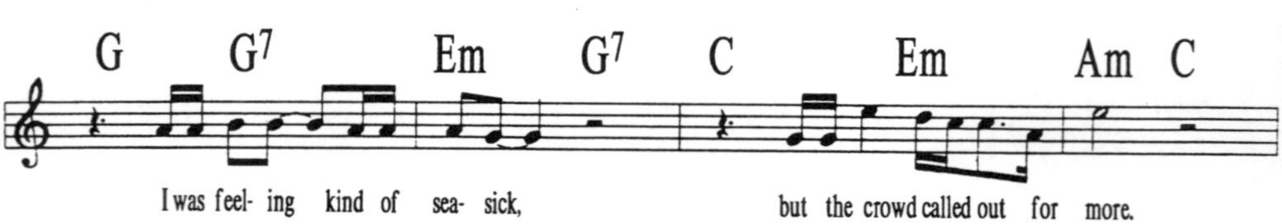

2. She said there is no reason, and the truth is plain to see,
But I wandered through my playing cards and would not let her be
One of sixteen Vestal Virgins who were leaving for the coast
And although my eyes were open they might just have well been closed.

BACKWATER BLUES

Traditional
Rhythmus: Blues
Tempo: Slow

2. When it thunders and it lightnings and the wind begins to blow,
When it thunders and it lightnings and the wind begins to blow,
There are thousands of people who ain't no place to go.

3. They rowed little boat about five miles 'cross the pond,
They rowed little boat about five miles 'cross the pond.
I packed all my things, throwed 'em in, and they rowed me along.

4. Then I went and stood upon some high old lonesome hill,
Then I went and stood upon some high old lonesome hill.
Then I looked down on the place where I used to live.

5. Backwater Blues done caused me pack my things and go,
Backwater Blues done caused me pack my things and go
'Cause my house felt down and I can't live there no more.

Banana Boat Song

Traditional
Interpret: Harry Belafonte
Rhythmus: Latin
Tempo: Moderato

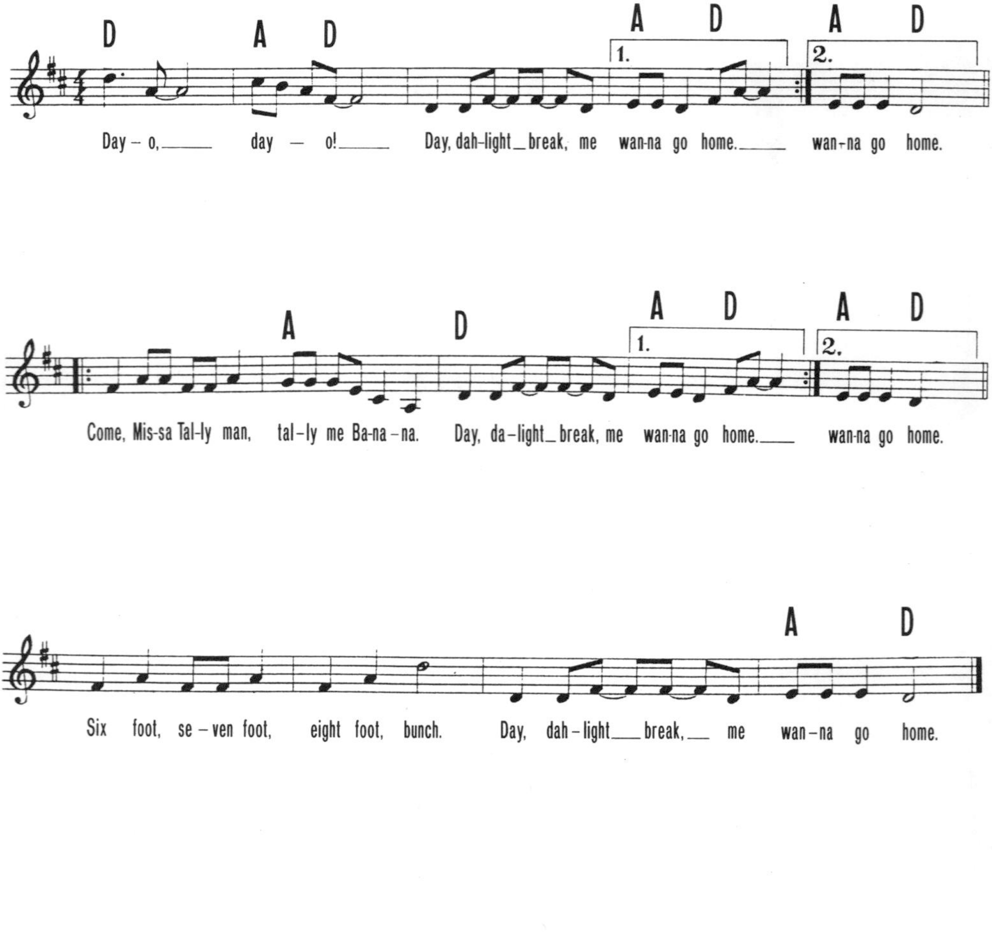

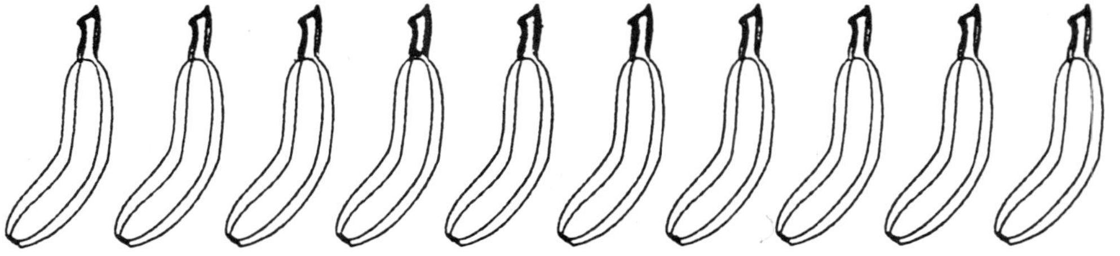

2. A clerk man a check, but him a check with caution.
Day, dah light break, me wanna go home.
Day-o, day-o! Day, dah light break, me wanna go home.
Day-o, day-o! Day, dah light break, me wanna go home.
Come Missa Tallyman, tally me Banana.
Day, dah light break, me wanna go home.
Come Missa Tallyman, tally me Banana.
Day, dah light break, me wanna go home.

3. My back just broke with bare exhaustion.
Day, dah light break, me wanna go home.
Day-o, day-o! Day, dah light break, me wanna go home.
Day-o, day-o! Day, dah light break, me wanna go home.
Come Missa Tallyman, tally me Banana.
Day, dah light break, me wanna go home.
Come Missa Tallyman, tally me Banana.
Day, dah light break, me wanna go home.

BEI MIR BIST DU *schön*

Text und Musik:
Sholom Secunda
Rhythmus: Medium Song
Tempo: Moderato

© 1937 by HARMS Inc., N.Y., Chappell International, London,
für Deutschland und Ostblock: Chappel&Co GmbH, Hamburg

E7 F7 E7 Am F7 E7
leis ein ver - lieb - ter Mil - lio - när. Du
mir bist Du schoen means that you're grand. Bei
Am
wirst es ja sehn: Bei mir bist Du schön, ich
mir bist Du schoen a - gain I'll ex - plain, it
E7 F7 E7 Am F7 E7 Am
schenk Dir ein Schloß und noch viel mehr. Ich nenn Dich
means you're the fair - est in the land. I could say
Dm Am
Bel - la, Bel - la, denn Dein Blick macht mich toll. Mein Herz schlägt
Bel - la, Bel - la e - ven say voon - der - bar; each lan - guage
Dm E7 E° E7
schnell und schnel - ler, denn Du küßt wun - der - voll. Bei
on - ly helps me tell you how grand you are. I've
Am
mir bist Du schön, ich muß es ge - stehn, viel
tried to ex - plain, bei mir bist Du schoen, so
E7 F7 E7 Am F7 E7 Am F7 E7 Am
1. 2.
schö - ner als al - les auf der Welt. Bei
kiss me and say you un - der - stand. Bei

BLAZE OF GLORY

Musik und Text:
Jon Bon Jovi
Interpret: Bon Jovi
Rhythmus: Rock Ballade
Tempo: Moderato

© Jon Bon Jovi Publishing/ PRI Music Inc.
Für D, A, CH: Polygram Songs Musikverlag GmbH

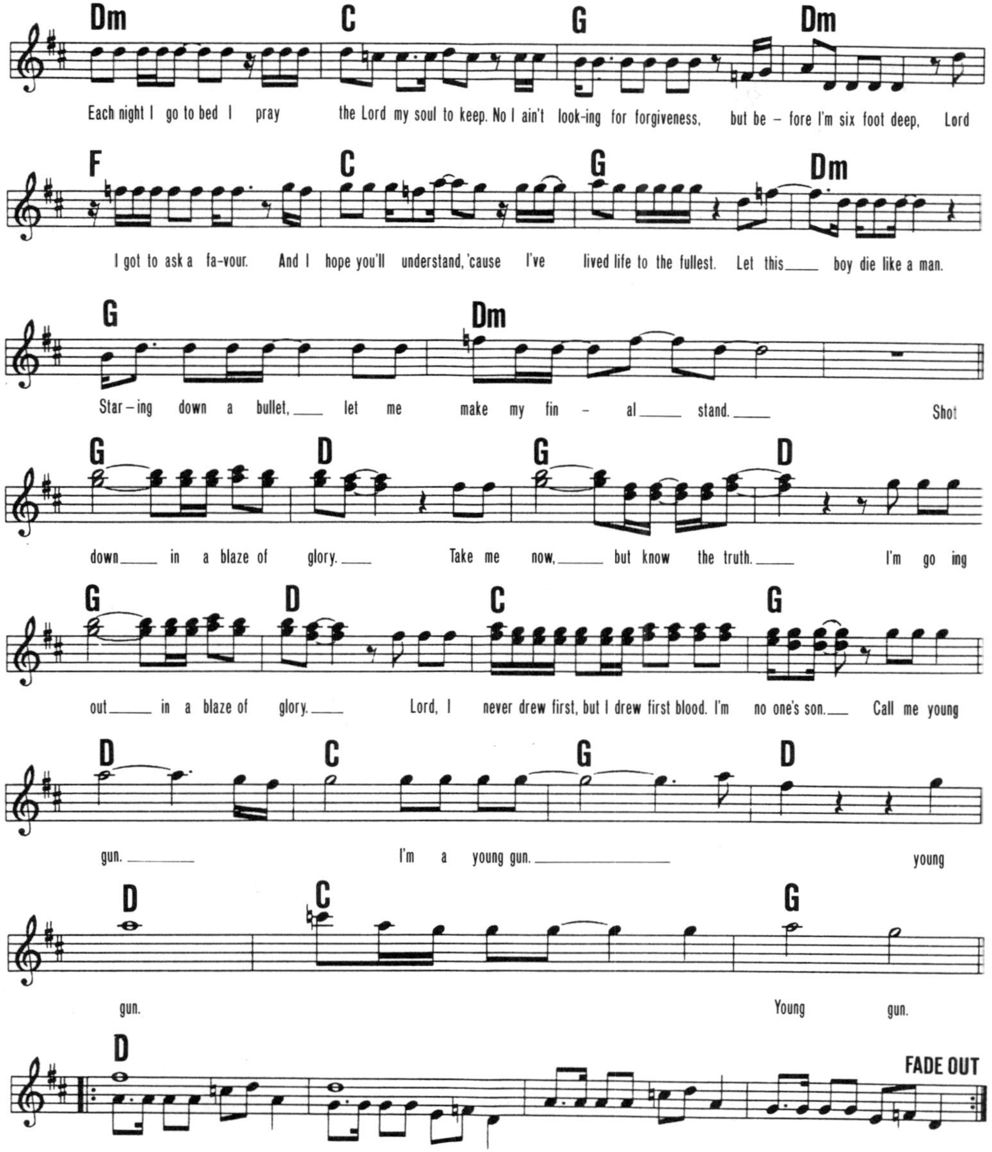

2. When you're brought into this world
They say you're born in sin
Well at least they gave me something
I didn't have to steal or have to win.
Well they tell me that I'm wanted
Yeah, I'm a wanted man
I'm a colt in your stable
I'm what Kain was to Able
Mister catch me if you can.

3. You ask about my concience
And I offer you my soul
You ask if I'll grow to be a wise man
Well I ask if I'll grow old
You ask me if I've known love
And what it's like to sing songs in the rain
Well I've seen love come
And I've seen it shot down
I've seen it die in vain.

4. Each night I go to bed
I pray the Lord my soul to keep
Now I ain't looking for forgiveness
But before I'm six foot deep
Lord I got to ask a favour
And I hope you'll understand
'Cause I've lived life to the fullest
Let this boy die like a man
Staring down a bullet, let me make my final stand.

Blowing in the wind

Musik und Text:
Bob Dylan
Interpreten: Bob Dylan, The Hollies
Rhythmus: Rock Ballade
Tempo: Moderato

© by M. Witmark & Sons, N.Y.
Für D, A, CH und Ostblock:
Neue Welt Musikverlag

2. How many times must a man look up
Before he can see the sky?
How many ears must one man have
Before he can hear people cry?
How many deaths will it take 'till he knows
That too many people have died?
The answer my friend , is blowing in the wind.
The answer is blowing in the wind.

3. How many years can a mountain exist
Before it is washed to the sea?
How many years can some people exist
Before they're allowed to be free?
How many times can a man turn his head
Pretend that he just doesn't see?
The answer my friend, is blowing in the wind.
The answer is blowing in the wind.

Blue Suede Shoes

Text und Musik: Carl Lee Perkins
Interpreten: Carl Lee Perkins, Elvis Presley, John Lennon
Rhythmus: Rock'n Roll
Tempo: Allegro

© by HI-LO Music, New York,
für Deutschland:
Musikverlag Intersong GmbH, Hamburg

do an – y – thing that you want to do, but uh uh hon-ey, lay off of my shoes, and don't
D7
A
you step on my blue suede shoes. Well you can
E7
A
1.
2.
do an – y – thing but lay off of my blue suede shoes. Well it's
A
blue, blue, blue suede shoes. Blue, blue, blue suede shoes, yeah,
D7
A
blue, blue, blue suede shoes. Blue, blue, blue suede shoes, yeah, you can
E7
A
A6
do an – y – thing but lay off of my blue suede shoes.

Born to be wild

Musik und Text:
Mars Bonfire
Interpreten: Steppenwolf
Rhythmus: Rock
Tempo: Allegro

© 1968 by Manitou Music, MCA Music GmbH, Hamburg
für D, A, CH und Ostblock

Rac-in' with the wind and the feel-in' that I'm un - der.
G6 A Em7 G6 A Em7
Yeah, dar-ling gon-na make it hap - pen. Take the world in a love em - brace.
G6 A Em7 G6 A Em7
Fire all of the guns at once and ex - plode in - to space. Like a
G6
true na - tures child I was born, born to be wild. We can
A G Em7
climb so high, I ne - ver want to die.
Em (E) D Em (E) D
Born to be wild
Em (E) D Em (E) D
Born to be wild
Em (E) D Em (E) D
Born to be wild

Bye, bye Love

Musik und Text:
Bryant, Boudleaux/ Bryant, Felice
Rhythmus: Rock'n Roll
Tempo: Allegro

© 1957 by Acuff Rose Opryland Music Inc.
Alle Rechte für D, A, CH und Ostblock bei
Neue Welt Musikverlag GmbH, München

C G C G
Bye bye, love, bye bye, hap - pi - ness
C G D7 G
Hel - lo, lone - li - ness. I think I'm gon - na cry.
C G C G
Bye bye, love. Bye bye, sweet car - ess
C G D7 G
Hel - lo, emp - ti - ness. I feel like I could die. Bye
D7 G G
1. 2.
bye my love bye bye

Chanson d'Amour

Text und Musik:
Wayne Shanklin
Rhythmus: Swing
Tempo: Moderato

© 1958 by Thunderbird Music Inc.,
Musikverlag Intersong GmbH, Hamburg

C7 F Gm C7
1.
da, more and more.
C7 F
2.
da, chan - son, chan - son d'a - mour. Ev' - ry time I
C7 F
hear chan - son, chan - son d'a - mour.

Clementine

Traditional
Rhythmus: Swing Feeling
Tempo: Allegro

2. Light she was and like a fairy, and her shoes were number nine.
Herring boxes without topses sandals were for Clementine.
Oh my darling, oh my darling, oh my darling Clementine ...

3. Drove she ducklings to the water every morning just at nine,
stubbed her toe against a splinter, fell into the foaming brine.
Oh my darling, oh my darling, oh my darling Clementine ...

4. Ruby lips above the water, blowing bubbles soft and fine,
but, alas, I was no swimmer, so I lost my Clementine.
Oh my darling, oh my darling, oh my darling Clementine ...

5. How I missed her, how I missed her, how I missed my Clementine,
till I kissed her little sister and forgot my Clementine.
Oh my darling, oh my darling, oh my darling Clementine ...

Daniel

Musik und Text:
Elton John/ Bernie Taupin
Interpret: Elton John
Rhythmus: Ballade
Tempo: Moderato

© 1972 by Dick James Music Ltd.
Für D, A, CH: Dick James Musikverlag GmbH

2. They say Spain is pretty,
Though I've never been;
Well Daniel says it's the best place
He's ever seen, oh, and
He should know, he's been there enough.
Lord, I miss Daniel,
Oh, I miss him so much.

down by the riverside

Traditional
Interpreten: Elvis Presley, Big Bill Broonzy
Rhythmus: Swing
Tempo: ♩ =186-190

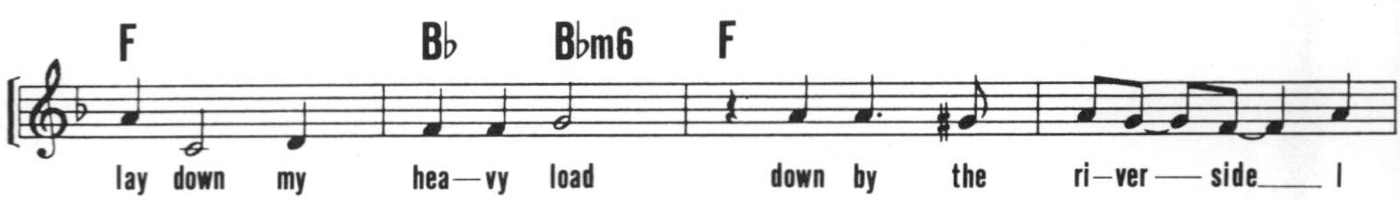

2. I'm gonna lay down my sword and shield
Down by the riverside...

3. I'm gonna lay down my travelin' shoes
Down by the riverside...

4. I'm gonna lay down my gun and belt
Down by the riverside...

5. I'm gonna put on my long white robe
Down by the riverside...

6. I'm gonna put on my stary crown
Down by the riverside...

7. I'm gonna walk with the Prince of Peace
Down by the riverside...

DREAMER

Musik und Text:
Roger Hodgsen/ Richard Davies
Interpreten: Supertramp
Rhythmus: Rock
Tempo: Allegro

© 1974 byRondor Music (London) Ltd.& Delicate Music Ltd..
Für D, A, CH Jugoslawien und osteuropäische Länder ex CSFR:
Rondor Musikverlag GmbH, Hamburg

A♭ B♭add9 Gm C
far out, what a day, a year, a life it is.
A♭ B♭add9 Gm
You know, well you know, you had it
C G Gm C
com - ing to you, now, there's not a lot I can do.
PIANO D A7sus4 A7 C Fmaj7 G D.S.
I said
PIANO D A7sus4 D

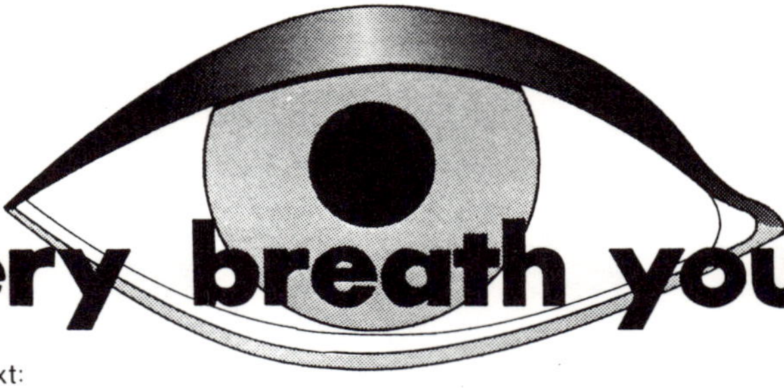

Every breath you take

Musik und Text:
Sting
Interpreten: Police, Sting
Rhythmus: Rock
Tempo: ♩=92

© by Bugle Songs Ltd.

C Dsus4 Em FINE
ev'- ry claim you stake, I'll be watch - ing you.
E♭ F
Since you've gone I've been lost with - out a trace. I dream at night I can on
E♭
ly see your face. I look a - round but it's you I can't re - place.
F E♭
I feel so cold and I long for your em - brace. I keep cry-ing ba - by, ba - by please.
G Em C Dsus4 Em
G Em
C Dsus4 Em D.S.
Oh, can't you

Five Hundred Miles

Traditional
Rhythmus: Medium Song
Tempo: Moderato

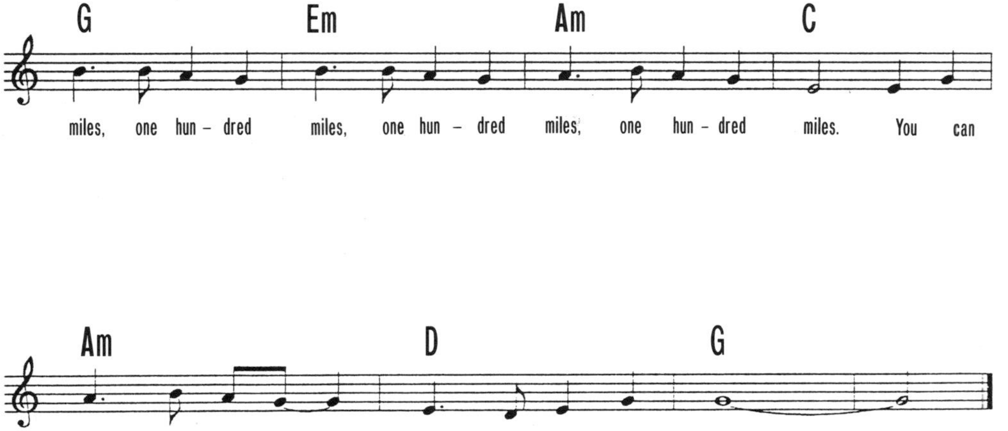

2. Lord I'm one, Lord I'm two,
Lord I'm three, Lord I'm four,
Lord I'm five hundred miles from home,
five hundred miles, five hundred miles,
Lord I'm five hundred miles from home.

3. Not a shirt on my back,
not a penny to my name,
Lord I can't go at home this way.
This way, this way, this way, this way,
Lord I can't go at home this way.

GET BACK

Musik und Text:
John Lennon/ Paul McCartney
Interpreten: Beatles
Rhythmus: Rock
Tempo: Moderato

© by Northern Songs Ltd.,
MCA Music GmbH, Hamburg für Deutschland,
Österreich, Schweiz und Ostblock

2. Sweet Loretta Martin thought she was a woman,
But she was another man.
All the girls around her say she's got it coming,
But she gets it while she can.

Give Peace a Chance

Musik und Text:
John Lennon
Interpreten: Plastic Ono Band, u.a.
Rhythmus: Medium Rock
Tempo: Moderato

© by Northern Songs Ltd.,
MCA Music GmbH, Hamburg für Deutschland,
Österreich, Schweiz und Ostblock

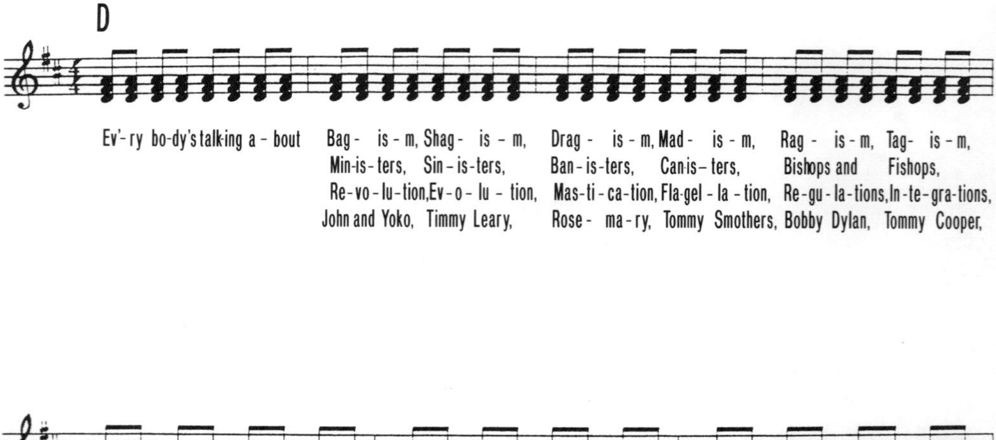

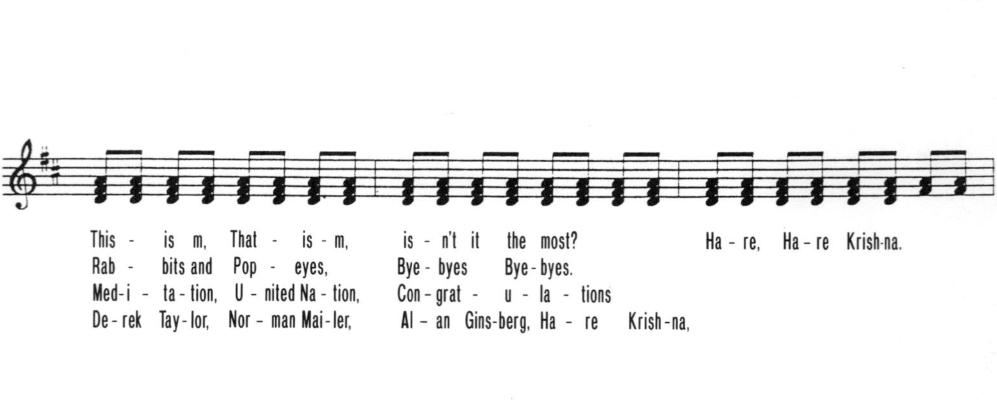

A7
All we are say - ing is
G F♯m A7 D
give peace a chance
A7
All we are say - ing is
G F♯m A7 D
give peace a chance

Gloria

Interpreten: Umberto Tozzi, Laura Branigan
Rhythmus: Bright Rock
Tempo: Allegro

© by "Sugar Musik"
Verlags GmbH, München

A E7 D A
wants you, why is-n't an-y-bo-dy call - ing? You___ don't have to
E7 G D E7
an - swer, leave them hang-ing on the line calling Glo-ri - a,___
A D E7
Glo - ri - a, I think they've got your
A E7
num - ber, I think they've got the a - li - as that you've been liv - ing
A F♯m H7
un - der. But you real - ly don't re - mem - ber, was it some-thing that they
E7 A D E7
said, or the voic-es in your head call - ing Glo-ri - a.___
A 1. 2. A E7
Glo-ri - a,
D A A E7 D A
Glo-ri - a. Glo-ri - a, Glo-ri - a.

Good Night Ladies

Traditional
Interpret: Lou Reed
Rhythmus: Swing
Tempo: fast, Allegro

2. Farewell, Ladies! Farewell, Ladies! Farewell, Ladies!
We're going to leave you now.
Merrily we roll along, roll along, roll along,
Merrily we roll along o'er the dark blue sea.

GUANTANAMERA

Traditional
Interpreten: José Feliciano, Sandpipers, Pete Seeger
Rhythmus: Latin
Tempo: ♩ =117

2. Guantanamera...
I write my rhymes with no learning,
And yet with truth they are burning,
But is the world waiting for them?
Or will they all just ignore them?
Have I a poet's illusion,
A dream to die in seclusion?

3. Guantanamera...
A little brook on a mountain,
The cooling spray of a fountain
Arouse in me an emotion,
More than the vast boundless ocean,
For there's a wealth beyond measure
In little things that we treasure.

4. Guananamera...
Yo soy un hombre sincero
De donde crece la palma,
Yo soy un hombre sincero
De donde crece la palma.
Yantes de morirme quiero,
Echarmis versos del alma.

Hello, Mary Lou

Originaltext und Musik: Gene Pitney
Deutscher Text: C. U. Blecher
Interpret: Ricky Nelson
Rhythmus: Shuffle
Tempo: Moderato

© 1960 by Six Continents Music Publ. Inc./
Champion Music Corp./
Chappell International Music Publ., London,
für Deutschland und Ostblockländer:
Chappell& Co GmbH, Hamburg/ MCA Music, Hamburg

A D
passed me by one sun – ny day, flashed those big brown eyes my way and
saw your lips, I heard your voice. Believe me, I just had no choice; wild
A E
ooh, I Wan – ted you for ev – er more. Now
hors – es could – n't make me stay a – way. I
A D
I'm not one that gets a – round.___ Swear my feet stuck to the ground___ and
thought a – bout a moon – lit – night,___ my arms a – bout you good and tight;___ that's
A E7 A D A A
1. 2.
though I ne – ver did___ meet you be – fore,___ I said "Hel – Hey, hey, hel –
all I had to see___ for me to say:___
A H7 E7 A D
So hel – lo, Ma – ry Lou, good – bye heart.
A H7 E7 A D A
Yes hel – lo, Ma – ry Lou, good – bye heart.

he's got the whole world in his hands

Traditional, Spiritual
Interpreten: Udo Jürgens, Mahalia Jackson
Rhythmus: Medium Song
Tempo: Moderato

2. He's got the tiny little baby in his hands.
He's got the tiny little baby in his hands.
He's got the tiny little baby in his hands.
He's got the baby in his hands.

3. He's got you and me brother in his hands.
He's got you and me brother in his hands.
He's got you and me brother in his hands.
He's got you and me in his hands.

4. He's got the son and his father in his hands.
He's got the son and his father in his hands.
He's got the son and his father in his hands.
He's got son and father in his hands.

5. He's got the mother and her daughter in his hands.
He's got the mother and her daughter in his hands.
He's got the mother and her daughter in his hands.
He's got mother and daughter in his hands.

6. He's got everybody here in his hands.
He's got everybody here in his hands.
He's got everybody here in his hands.
He's got everybody in his hands.

7. He's got the sun and the moon in his hands.
He's got the sun and the moon in his hands.
He's got the sun and the moon in his hands.
He's got sun and moon in his hands.

HEY JUDE

Musik und Text:
John Lennon/ Paul McCartney
Interpreten: Beatles, Paul McCartney
Rhythmus: Rock Ballade
Tempo: Slow

© by Northern Songs Ltd.,
MCA Music GmbH, Hamburg für Deutschland,
Österreich, Schweiz und Ostblock

2. Hey Jude, don't be afraid,
You were made to go out and get her.
The minute, you let her under your skin,
Then you begin to make it better.
So let it out and let it in,
Hey Jude, begin,
You're waiting for someone to perform with.
And don't you know that it's just you,
Hey Jude, you'll do.
The movement you need is on your shoulder.

3. Hey Jude, don't let me down,
You have found her, now go and get her.
Remember to let her into your heart,
Then you can start to make it better.

HIROSHIMA

Text und Musik:
Dave Morgan
Interpreten:Wishful Thinking, Sandra
Rhythmus:Ballade, Funk Rock
Tempo: Moderato

© 1971 by Global Music Inc.
Für D, A, CH: Global Musikverlag, München

G D Am C D
1.
And the world re - mem-bers his face,__ re - mem-bers the place__was here.
And the world re - mem-bers his face,__ re - mem-bers the flame__was here.
D Am (D) Em Am (D)
2.
Hi__ - __ ro - shi - ma. Hi__ - __ ro
Em Am (D) Em
shi - ma. Hi__ - __ ro - shi - ma.

Traditional
Interpretin: Nina Hagen
Rhythmus: Funk Rock
Tempo: Moderato

Hm C♯m F♯
I tend to here, I tend to there, then I don't know
F♯7 Hm E7
(I don't know) then some-times, Lord, you know, it hurt bey-ond com-
A7 D.S.
pare. Hold me Lord

IMAGINE

Text und Musik:
John Lennon
Interpret: John Lennon
Rhythmus: Medium Rock
Tempo: Moderato

© 1971 by Northern Songs Ltd. Ass.
1984 to Lenono Music, USA.
Für D, A, CH, PL, CSFR, H, YU, R, BG, UdSSR:
Nordton Musikverlag GmbH, Berlin

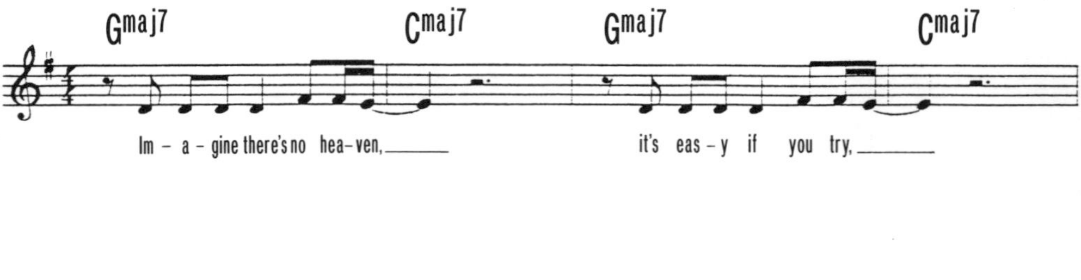

2. Imagine there's no countries,
It isn't hard to do,
Nothing to kill or die for,
And no religion too.
Imagine all the people
Living life in peace.
You may say I'm a dreamer,
But I'm not the only one,
I hope some day you'll join us,
And the world will be as one.

3. Imagine no possessions,
I wonder if you can,
No need for greed or hunger,
A brotherhood of man.
Imagine all the people
Sharing all the world.
You may say I'm a dreamer,
But I'm not the only one,
I hope some day you'll join us,
And the world will live as one.

I shot the Sheriff

Musik und Text:
Bob Marley
Interpreten: Eric Clapton, Bob Marley
Rhythmus: Reggae
Tempo: Moderately slow

*© 1974 by CAYMAN Music Inc., USA.
Für D, A, CH: Rolf Budde GmbH & Co
Musikverlag KG, Berlin*

2. I shot the sheriff,
But I swear it was in self-defense.
I shot the sheriff,
But I swear it was in self-defense.
Freedom came my way one day,
And I started out of town.
All of a sudden, I see sheriff John Brown
Aiming to shoot me down.
So I shot, I shot him down.
But I say: ...

3. I shot the sheriff,
But I swear it was in self-defense.
I shot the sheriff,
But I swear it was in self-defense.
Sheriff John Brown always hated me;
For what I don't know.
Every time that I plant a seed,
He said: "Kill it before it grows!"
He sais: "Kill it before it grows!"
But I say: ...

4. I shot the sheriff,
But I swear it was in self-defense.
I shot the sheriff,
But I swear it was in self-defense.
Reflexes got the better of me,
And what is to be must be.
Every day, the bucket goes to the well,
But one day the bottom will drop out.
Yes one day the bottom will drop out.
But I say: ...

John Brown's Body

Traditional
Interpreten: The Lords
Rhythmus: Swing
Tempo: ♩ =176

2. The stars of heaven are looking kindly down
On the grave of old John Brown.

3. He's gone to be a soldier in the army of the Lord,
And his soul is marching on.

4. John Brown's knapsack is strapp'd upon his back,
And his soul is marching on.

5. His pet lambs will meet him on the way,
And they'll go marching on.

6. We'll hang Jeff Davis on a sour apple tree,
As we go marching on.

Glory, glory hallelujah, glory, glory hallelujah,
Glory, glory hallelujah, his soul is marching on.

Joshua fought the battle of Jericho

Spiritual
Interpreten: Elvis Presley, Les Humphries Singers
Rhythmus: Swing
Tempo: ♩=180

2. When the chillun of Israel begin to march
Seven times roun' an' roun'
Ol' Joshua commanded de sun to stan' still,
An' de sun did never go down 'dat mornin'

3. Den de lamram sheep horns begin to blow,
Trumpets begin to soun'
Ol' Joshua commanded de Chillun to shout,
An' de walls came tumblin' down 'dat mornin'

LADY in BLACK

Musik und Text:
K. Hensley
Interpreten: Uriah Heep
Rhythmus: Rock Ballade
Tempo: Moderato

© 1970 by EMI Music (Brow Ass.)
Für D, A, CH: Fanfare Musikverlag, München

2. She asked me name my foe then!
I said the need within some men
To fight and kill their brothers
Whithout thought of love or god.
And I begged her give me horses
To trample down my enemy
So eager was my passion
To be far of this waste of life.

3. But she would not think of battle
That reduces men to animals
So easy to begin
And yet impossible to end.
For she is the mother of all men
Did counsel me so wisely then
I feared to walk alone again
And asked if she would stay.

4. Oh, Lady lend your hand, I cried
Or let me rest here at your side
Have faith and trust in me she said
And filled my heart with life.
There is no strength in numbers
Have no such misconception
But when you need me, be asured
I won't be far away.

Let it be

Musik und Text:
John Lennon/ Paul McCartney
Interpreten: Beatles
Rhythmus: Rock Ballade
Tempo: ♩=70

© by Northern Songs Ltd.,
MCA Music GmbH, Hamburg für Deutschland,
Österreich, Schweiz und Ostblock

2. And when the broken-hearted people, living in the world agree,
There will be an answer, let it be.
For though they may be parted, there is still a chance that they will see,
There will be an answer, let it be.
Let it be, let it be, let it be, let it be.
There will be an answer, let it be.

3. And when the night is cloudy, there is still a light that shines on me,
Shine until tomorrow, let it be.
I wake up to the sound of music, mother Mary comes to me,
Speaking words of wisdom, let it be.
Let it be, let it be, let it be, let it be.
Whisper words of wisdom, let it be.

Let's dance

Text und Musik:
David Bowie
Interpret: David Bowie
Rhythmus: Funk
Tempo: Moderato

© by Jones Music, USA.
Rechte für D, A, CH und osteuropäische Länder:
EMI Music Publishing Germany GmbH, Hamburg

G C D C D
If you say hide, we'll hide, be –
G Em7 C D
cause my love for you would break my heart in two. If
Am
you should fall in – to my arms and trem – ble like a flow – er. Let's
Am11 Am6
dance, for fear your grace should fall. Let's
F6 Am
dance, for fear your grace should fall. Let's
Am11 Am6
sway, you could look in – to my eyes. Let's
F6 Am D.S.
sway under the moon-light, the ser – i – ous moon-light.
Am11 Am6
dance. Put on your red shoes and dance the blues. Let's
F6 Am FADE OUT
dance

Let's spend the night together

Text und Musik:
Mick Jagger, Keith Richards
Interpreten: Rolling Stones, Roger Chapman
Rhythmus: Rock
Tempo: Moderato

© by Mirage Music Ltd.
für D, A, CH: Essex Musikvertrieb GmbH

C
Let's spend the night together now. Let's spend the night together.
G C
Now I need you more than ev - er
G C
You know I'm smil - ing ba - by. You need some guid - ing ba - by.
G D7
I need you by me ba - by. I need you more than ev - er.
Let's spend the night to - ge - ther. Let's spend the night to - ge - ther now.
G Hm D7 G Hm
Yeah. Yeah.
D7 G Hm D7
I need you ba - by. Yeah. More
G Hm D7
than ev - er now. Yeah. More than ev - er now.
G Hm D7
Oh, yeah, su - gar. More than ev - er now.
G Hm D7
D7
Let's spend the night to - ge - ther. Now I need you more than ev - er

LIGHT my FIRE

Musik und Text:
Morrison/ Manzarek/ Krieger/ Densmore
Interpreten: Doors, José Feliciano
Rhythmus: Rock Ballade
Tempo: Medium fast

© 1969 by Doors Music Co.
Für D, A, CH: Global Musikverlag, München

Am F♯m Am F♯m
know that it would be un – true. You know that I would be a liar.
Am F♯m Am F♯m
If I was to say to you, girl we could-n't get much higher.
G A D G A D
Come on ba-by, light my fire. Come on bă-by, light my fire.
F C D F C D
Try to set the night on fire. Try to set the night on fire.
F C D F C D
Try to set the night on fire. Try to set the night on fire.
ORGEL
G D F B♭ E♭ A♭ A

Little Brown Jug

Traditional
Musik: R.A. Eastburn
Rhythmus: Latin
Tempo: Moderato

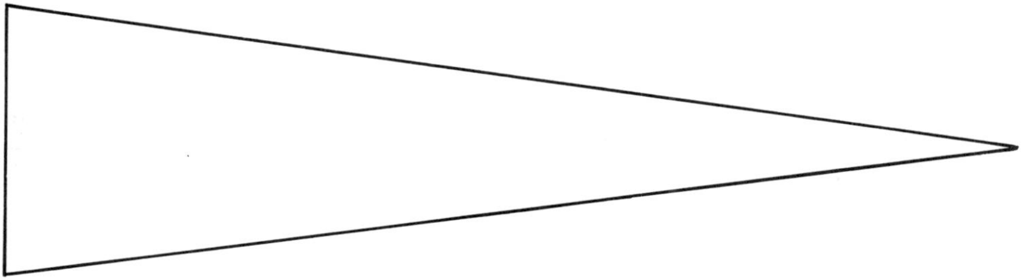

2. 'Tis you who makes my friends my foes,
'Tis you who makes me wear old clothes;
Here you are, so near my nose,
So tip her up and down she goes.

3. Whwn I go toiling to my farm
I take a little brown jug under my arm;
I place it under a shady tree-
Little brown jug, 'tis you and me.

4. If I'd a cow that gave such milk,
I'd clothe her in the finest silk;
I'd feet her on the choicest hay,
And milk her forty times a day.

5. If all the folks in Adam's race
were gathered together in one place;
Then I'd prepare to shed a tear,
Before I'd part from you, my dear.

6. The rose is red, my nose is, too
The violet's blue and so are you;
And yet I guess, before I stop,
We'd better take another drop.

Locomotive Breath

Musik und Text:
Ian Anderson
Interpreten: Jethro Tull
Rhythmus: Rock
Tempo: Moderato

© by Ian Anderson Music/
Chrysalis Music Ltd.
Für D, A, CH: EMI Music Publishing Germany GmbH, Hamburg

2. He sees his children jumping off at stations one by one.
His woman and his best friend in bed and having fun.
Oh, he's crawling down the corridor on his hands and his knees.
Old Charlie stole the handle, and the train...

3. He hears the silence howling, catches angels as they fall,
And the alltime winner has got him by the balls.
Oh, he picks up Gideon's Bible; open at page one.
I thank God he stole the handle, and the train...

looking for Freedom

Text und Musik:
Jack White/ Gary Cowtan
Interpret: David Hasselhoff
Rhythmus: Moderato Rock
Tempo: Allegro

© 1978 by Young Musikverlag GmbH/ RMI

Am F C
when you re-a-lize the freedom money buys__ you'll come running home____ some_day.________
I've been look-in' for free – dom,____ I've been look-in' so____ long.
Am G C
I've been look-in' for free – dom,____ still the search__ goes on.
F C
I paid a lot-ta dues, had plenty to lose,__ travell-ing a cross the land,___
F
worked on a farm,__ got some mus-cle in my arm____ but still I'm not a self-made man. I'll
C Am F C
be on the run__ for many years to__ come. I'll be searching door to______ door,__ but
Am F C
giv-en sometime,_ some day I'm gonna find___ the freedom I've been search – ing_for.___
I've been lookin' for free – dom,____ I've been lookin' so____ long.
Am G C
I've been lookin' for free – dom,____ still the search__ goes on.

MACKIE MESSER

Text: Bertolt Brecht
Musik: Kurt Weill aus: "Die Dreigroschenoper"
Rhythmus: Ballade

© 1928, 1956 by Universal Edition A.G., Wien

Am Am7 Dm
Kai geht Mak – kie Mes – ser, der von
Dm7 G7 C6
al – lem nichts ge – wußt. Und das
C6 Dm
gro – ße Feu – er in So – ho, sie – ben
G9 C6
Kin – der und ein Greis, in der
Am Am7 Dm
Men – ge Mak – kie Mes – ser, den man nichts
Dm7 G7 C6
fragt und der nichts weiß. Und die
C6 Dm
min – der jähr' – ge Wit – we, de – ren
G9 C6
Na – men je – der weiß, wach – te
Am Am7 Dm
auf und war ge – schän – det, Mak – kie
Dm7 G7 C6
wel – ches war Dein Preis? Wach – te
Am Am7 Dm
auf und war ge – schän – det, Mak – kie
Dm7 G7 C6
wel – ches war Dein Preis?

MASSACHUSETTS

Musik und Text:
Barry, Robin und Maurice Gibb
Interpreten: Bee Gees
Rhythmus: Ballade
Tempo: Moderato

© 1967 by Gibb Brothers Music
Musik-Edition Discoton GmbH (BMG UFA Musikverlage), München,
für D, A, CH, Polen, CSFR, Ungarn, Rumänien, Bulgarien,
Jugoslawien, UdSSR, Albanien

2. Tried to hitch a ride to San Francisco;
Gotta do the things I wanna do.
And the lights all went out in Massachusets
The day I left her standing on her own.

3. Talk about the life in Massachusets;
Speak about the people I have seen.
And the lights all went down in Massachusets;
And Massachusets is one place I have seen.

MATERIAL GIRL

Musik und Text:
Peter Brown/ Robert S. Rans
Interpretin: Madonna
Rhythmus: Rock
Tempo: Moderato

© 1984, 1985 by Minong Publ. Co.
Alle Rechte für D, A, CH und Ostblock
bei: Neue Welt Musikverlag GmbH, München

2. Some boys romance, some boys slow dance.
That's all right with me.
If they can't raise my int'rest then I have to let them be.
Some boys try and some boys lie but I don't let them play.
Only boys who save their pennies make my rainy day.
Boys may come and boys may go and that's alright with me.
Experience has made me rich and now they're after me.

matilda

Musik und Text:
SPAN, Norman
Interpret: Harry Belafonte
Rhythmus: Latin
Tempo: ♩ =126

(C) 1953 by DUCHESS MUSIC CORP.
für Deutschland, Österreich, Schweiz:
HERMANN SCHNEIDER BÜHNEN- UND MUSIKVERLAGS KG, Wien
für Deutschland:
HERMANN SCHNEIDER BÜHNEN- UND MUSIKVERLAGS KG, Wien
& EDITION PRIMUS ROLF BUDDE KG, Berlin

2. Well the money was just inside me bed. Stuck in the
Pillow beneath me head. Matilda she take me money and,
Run Venezuela.

3. Well, me friends never to love again. All me money
Gone in vain, Matilda she take me money and,
Run Venezuela.

Michael Row Your Boat Ashore

Traditional
Interpreten: Joan Baez, Sandpipers
Rhythmus: Swing
Tempo: Moderato

2. Michael's boat is a music boat, Hallelujah.
Michael's boat is a music boat, Hallelujah

3. Sister help to trim the sail, Hallelujah.
Sister help to trim the sail, Hallelujah.

4. Jordan's river is deep and wide, Hallelujah.
Meet my mother on the other side, Hallelujah.

5. Jordan's river is chilly and cold, Hallelujah.
Kills a body but not the soul, Hallelujah.

MIDNIGHT SPECIAL

Traditional
Interpreten: Spencer Davis Group, CCR, Harry Belafonte
Rhythmus: Medium Rock
Tempo: Allegro

2. If you ever go to Houston, you better walk right;
You better not stagger, you better not fight;
Sheriff Benson will arrest you, he'll carry you down,
And if the jury finds you guilty, penitentiary bound.

3. Yondèr come little Rosie, how in the world do you know,
I can tell her by her apron, and the dress she wore.
Umbrella on her shoulder, Piece of paper in her hand,
She goes a-marching to the captain, says I want my man.

Mighty Quinn

Text und Musik:
Bob Dylan
Interpreten: Bob Dylan, Manfred Mann
Rhythmus: Rock
Tempo: Moderato

© 1968 by Dwarf Music.
Alle Rechte für D, A, CH und Ostblock bei
Neue Welt Musikverlag GmbH, München

2. I like to do just like the rest,
I like my sugar sweet,
But guarding fumes and making haste.
It ain't my cup of meet,
Ev'rybody's 'neath the trees,
Feeding pidgeons on a limb,
But when Quinn the eskimo gets here,
All the pidgeons gonna run to him.

Moonlight Shadow

Musik und Text:
Mike Oldfield
Interpreten: Mike Oldfield Band
Rhythmus: Medium Rock
Tempo: Allegro

© 1983 by Virgin Music (Pubs) Ltd.
Alle Rechte für D, A, CH: Virgin Music Publishers Germany

2. The trees that whisper in the evening,
Carried away by a moonlight shadow.
Sing a song of sorrow and grieving,
Carried away by a moonlight shadow.
All she saw was the silhouette of a gun
Far away on the other side.
He was shot six times by a man on the run
And she couldn't find how to push through.

3. Four a.m. in the morning, carried away by a moonlight shadow.
I watch your vision forming, carried away by a moonlight shadow.
The stars move slowly in a silvery light far away on the other side.
Will you come to talk to me this night,
But she couldn't find how to push through.
Caught in the middle of a hundred and five
The night was heavy and the air was alive
But she couldn't find how to push through.

MY BONNIE IS OVER THE OCEAN

Traditional
Interpreten: Tony Sheridan, Beatles
Rhythmus: Swing
Tempo: Allegro

2. Oh, blow ye winds over the ocean,
Oh, blow ye winds over the sea,
Oh, blow ye winds over the ocean,
And bring back my bonnie to me!
Bring back ...

3. The wind has blown over the ocean,
The wind has blown over the sea,
The wind has blown over the ocean,
And brought back my bonnie to me.
Brought back ...

4. Last night as I lay on my pillow,
Last night as I lay on my bed.
Last night as I lay on my pillow,
I dreamt that my bonnie was dead.
Bring back ...

1999

Musik und Text:
Roger Nelson
Interpret: Prince
Rhythmus: Medium Rock
Tempo: Allegro

© 1980 by Controversy Music.
Für D, A, CH und Ost-Europa:
Edition Intro Gebr. Meisel GmbH

2. I was dreamin' when I wrote this,
So sue me if I go too fast;
But life is just a party,
And parties weren't meant to last.
War is all around us,
My mind says prepare to fight.
So if I gotta die I'm gonna
Listen to my body tonight.

3. If you didn't come to party,
Don't bother knockin' on the door.
I've got a lion in my pocket,
And, baby, he's ready to roar.
Ev'rybody's got a bomb,
We could all die any day;
But before I'll let that happen,
I'll dance my life away.

OH SUSANNA

Traditional
Interpreten: Janis Joplin, The Byrds
Rhythmus: Rock
Tempo: Allegro

2. I had a dream the other night, when everything was still.
I dreamed I saw Susanna a-coming down the hill.

3. A red red rose was in her cheek, a tear was in her eye,
I said to her, Susanna girl, Susanna don't you cry.

ONE MORE NIGHT

Musik und Text:
Phil Collins
Interpret: Phil Collins
Rhythmus: Ballade
Tempo: Moderately slow

© 1984 by Philip Collins Ltd./ Hit+Run Music Publ. Ltd.
Alle Rechte für D, A, CH bei Virgin Music Publishers, Germany

2. I've been sitting here so long, wasting time, just staring at the phone.
And I was wond'ring should I call you, then I thought maybe you're not alone.
Give me one more night. Give me just one more night,
Oh, one more night, 'cause I can't wait forever.

3. I know there'll never be a time you'll ever feel the same.
And I know it's only words. But if you change your mind,
You know that I'll be here, and maybe we both can learn.

People are People

Musik und Text:
Martin L. Gore
interpretiert von Depeche Mode
Rhythmus: Techno Pop
Tempo: ♩ =110

© by Sonet Publ. Ltd., London.
Für D, A, CH:
Edition Manito c/o Global Musikverlag, München

2. ...Now you're punching and you're kicking and you're shouting at me,
And I'm relying on your common decency.
So far it hasn't surfaced but I'm sure it exists,
It just takes a while to travel from your head to your fists.

Plaisir d'Amour

Traditional
Interpreten: Judy Collins, Elvis Presley
Rhythmus: Walzer
Tempo: Moderato

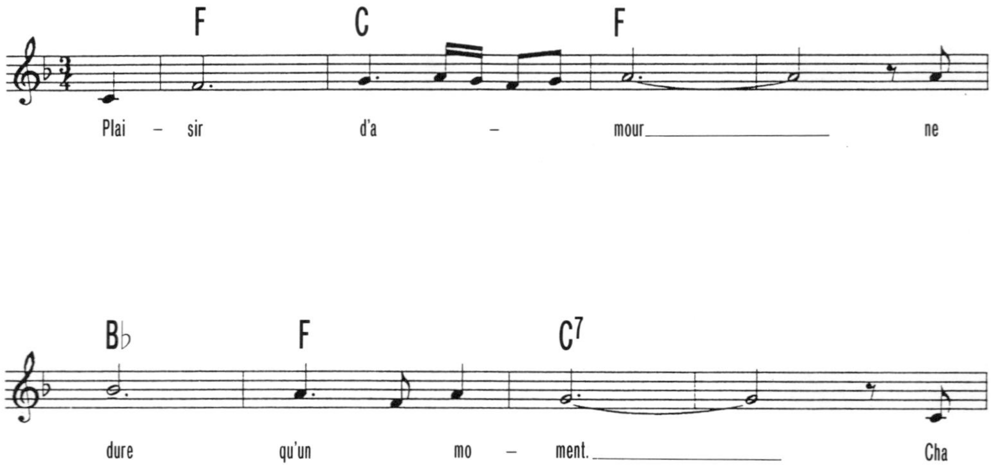

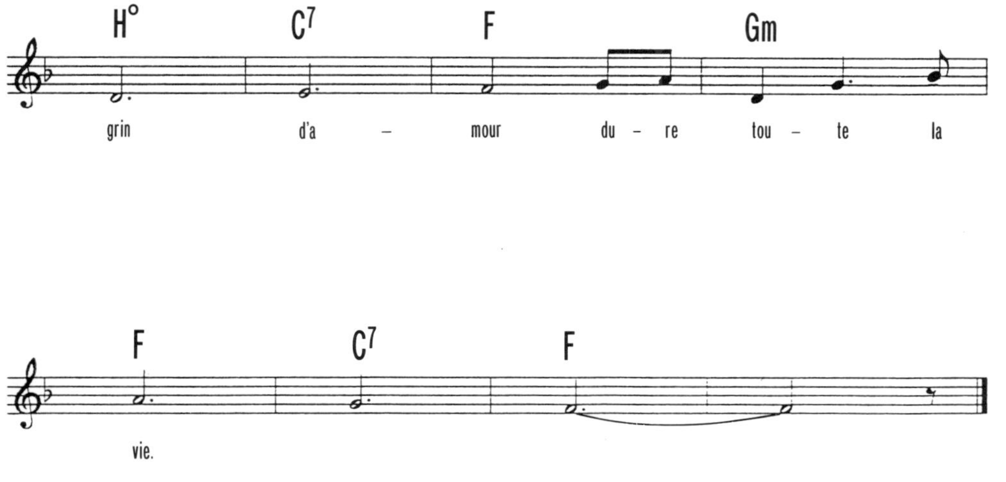

2. The joys of love are but a moment long,
The pain of love endures the whole life.

3. Your eyes kissed mine, I saw the love in them shine,
You brought me heaven right then when your eyes kissed mine.

4. My love loves me, and all the wonders I see,
A rainbow shines in my window, my love loves me.

5. And now he's gone, like a dream that fades into dawn,
But the words stay locked in my heartstrings, "My love loves me"

(Red River Valley)

Traditional
Interpreten: Johnny and the Hurricanes
Rhythmus: Rock
Tempo: Moderato

2. Oh, just think of the valley you're leaving
Oh, how lonely, how sad it will be;
And just think of the fond heart you're breaking,
And the grief you are causing to me.

3. Come and sit by my side if you love me,
Do not hasten to bid me adieu;
But remember the Red River Valley
And the girl that has loved you so true.

RIVERS OF Babylon

Traditional
Interpreten: Boney M.
Rhythmus: Reggae
Tempo: Moderato

D A7 D
How___ can___ we sing king Al – fa___ song in a strange land.
A7 D
So that the words of our___ mouth and___ the me-di – ta – tion of our___
A7 D A7 D
heart be ac – cept – a – ble in thy___ sight o – ver I.

Rock around the clock

Musik und Text:
Max C. Freedman/ Jimmy de Knight
interpretiert von Bill Haley
Rhythmus: Rock
Tempo: ♩ =168

© by E. Kassner & Co. Musikverlag

2. When the clock strikes two,
Three and four,
If the band slows down
We'll yell for more,
We're gonna rock ...

3. When the chimes rings five,
Six and seven,
We'll be right
In seventh heaven,
We're gonna rock ...

4. When it's eight, nine, ten,
Eleven too,
I'll be goin' strong
And so are you,
We're gonna rock ...

5. When the clock strikes twelve,
We'll cool off then,
Start a-rockin' 'round
The clock again.
We're gonna rock ...

Sailing

Musik und Text:
Gavin Sutherland
Interpret: Rod Stewart
Rhythmus: Ballade
Tempo: Slow

© 1972 by Island Music Ltd..
Für D, A, CH: Polygram Songs Musikverlag GmbH

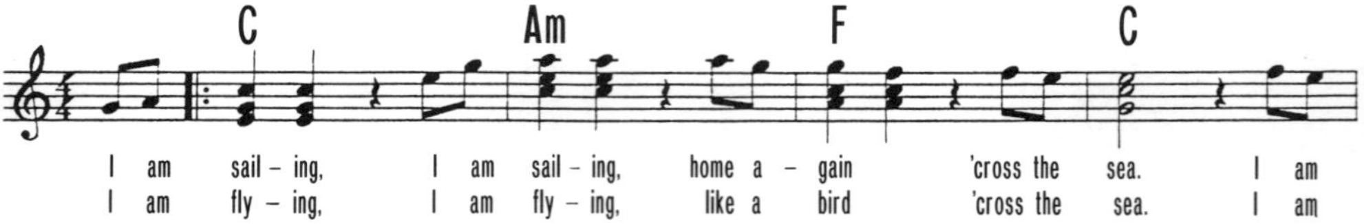

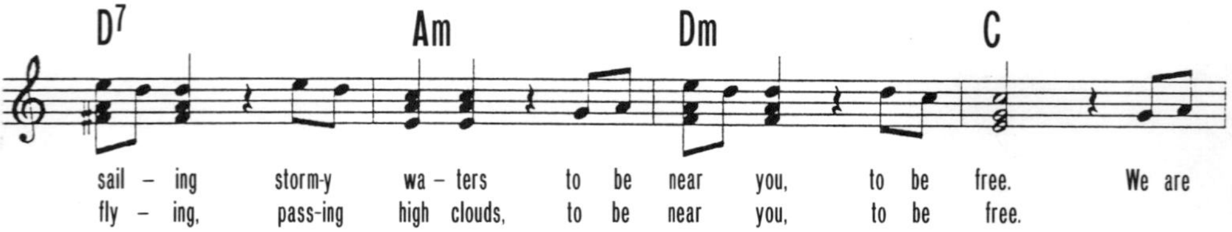

D7 Am Dm C
sail – ing stormy-y wa – ters, to be near you, to be free. To be
Dm C
near you, to be free.

Satisfaction

Musik und Text:
Mick Jagger/ Keith Richards
Interpreten: Rolling Stones
Rhythmus: Rock
Tempo: ♩ =130

© by Mirace Music Ltd., London.
Für D, A, CH: Essex Musikvertrieb GmbH, Köln

2. When I'm watchin' my TV
And a man comes on and tells me
"How white my shirts can be" 'Cause he doesn't smoke
But he (ah) can't be a man The same cigarettes as me.

3. When I'm ridin' 'round the world
And I'm doing this and I'm signin' that
And I'm tryin' to make some girl Maybe next week" Can't you see
She tell me (ah) "Baby better come back I'm on a loosing streak.

SGT. PEPPER'S Lonely Hearts Club Band

Musik und Text:
John Lennon, Paul McCartney
Interpreten: Beatles, Jimi Hendrix
Rhythmus: Medium Rock
Tempo: Allegro

© by Northern Songs Ltd.,
MCA Music GmbH, Hamburg für Deutschland,
Österreich, Schweiz und Ostblock

2. I don't really want to stop the show, but I thought you might like to know, that the singer is going to sing a song,
And he wants you all to sing along. So may I introduce to you the one and only Billy Shears ...

SHOUT

Musik und Text:
Roland Orzabal/ Ian Stanley
Interpreten: Tears for Fears
Rhythmus: Rock
Tempo: Medium

© 1989 by Virgin Music (Pubs) Ltd./ 10 Music Ltd.
Alle Rechte für D, A, CH bei
Virgin Music Publishers, Germany

2. They gave you life,
And in return you gave them hell.
As cold as ice, I hope we live to tell the tale.

Smoke on the water

Musik und Text:
Jon Lord/ Ritchie Blackmore/
Ian Gillan/ Roger Glover/ Ian Paice
Interpreten: Deep Purple
Rhythmus: Rock
Tempo: Moderato

© by B. Feldman & Co Ltd. t/as HEC Music.
Rechte für D, A, CH und osteuropäische Länder:
EMI Music Publishing Germany GmbH, Hamburg

2. They burned the gambling house, it died with an awful sound, Funky Claude was running in and out, pulling kiss out the ground.
When it all was over, we had to find another place, but swiss time was running out, it seemed that we would loose the race.

3. It was empty, cold and bare, but with the Rolling Stones thing're just outside. but makin' our music there with a
Few red lights, a few old beds we made a place to sweet, no matter what we get out of this, I know, I know we'll never forget.

STAIRWAY TO HEAVEN

Text und Musik:
Jimmy Page/ Robert Plant
Interpreten: Led Zeppelin
Rhythmus: Rock Ballade
Tempo: Slow

© 1972 by Superhype Publishing.
Alle Rechte für D, A, CH und Ostblock bei:
Musik unserer Zeit Verlag GmbH, München

2. And it's whispered that soon if we all call the tune, then the piper will lead us to reason.
And a new day will dawn for those who stand long and the forrests will echo with laughter. Ooh, ...
Yes, there are two paths you can go by but in the long run, there's still time to change the road you're on.
Dear lady, can you hear the wind blow, and did you know your stairway lies on the whispering wind.

STAND *by me*

Text und Musik: Ben E. King/ Elmo Glick
Interpret: Ben E. King, John Lennon
Rhythmus: Slow Rock
Tempo: Moderato

© by 1961 by Progressive Music Publ.,
Trio Music Co.
Für Deutschland:
Musikverlag Intersong GmbH, Hamburg

D E7 A
is the on – ly___ light we'll___ see, no I won't___
tain should crum – ble___ to the___ sea, I won't cry,___
F♯m
be a – fraid,___ oh, I___ won't be a – fraid, just as long___
I won't cry,___ no, I___ won't shed a tear
D E7 A
as you stand,___ stand by me.___ So dar – lin, dar – lin,
A F♯m
stand___ by___ me, oh,___ stand___ by___ me. Oh,___
D E7 A
FINE/FADE OUT
stand,___ stand by___ me.___ Stand by___ me. 2. If the sky

Strangers in the night

Musik: Bert Kämpfert
Interpreten: Frank Sinatra u.a.
Rhythmus: Medium Swing
Tempo: Moderato

© 1966 by Champion Music Corp. & Roosevelt Music Co. New York.
MCA Music GmbH, Hamburg für D, A, CH und Ostblock

D9 G (G7/F# G7/F)
some–thing in my heart told me I must have you.
Dm6 E9♭
Strangers in the night, two lonely peo–ple we were stran-gers in the night, up to the mo–ment when we
Am Cm G Em7 Am7 D7
said our first hel–lo, lit–tle did we know, love was just a glance a-way, a warm em-brac-ing dance a–way and
G
ev–er since that night we've been to-ge – ther, lo – vers at first sight, in love for ev – er.
D7 Am7 D7 G6
It turned out so right for stran–gers in the night.

SUMMERTIME

Musik: G. Gershwin
Text: Du Bose Hayward/ I. Gershwin
aus: "Porgy&Bess"
Interpreten: Janis Joplin u.a.
Rhythmus: Ballade/ Musical Song
Tempo: Moderato

© 1935 by Gershwin Publ. Co., N.Y./
Warner Chappell International, London.
Für Deutschland und Ostblockländer:
Chappell&Co GmbH, Hamburg

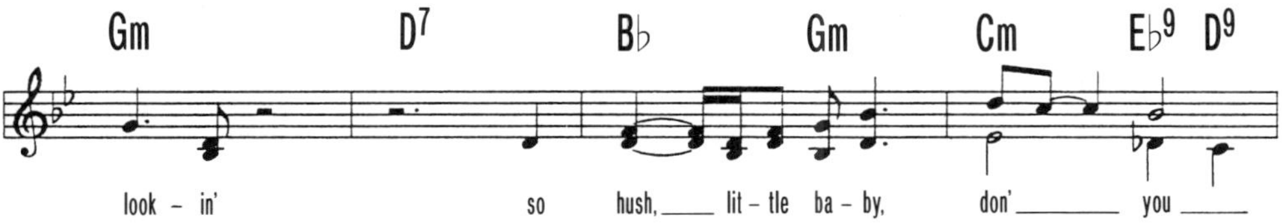

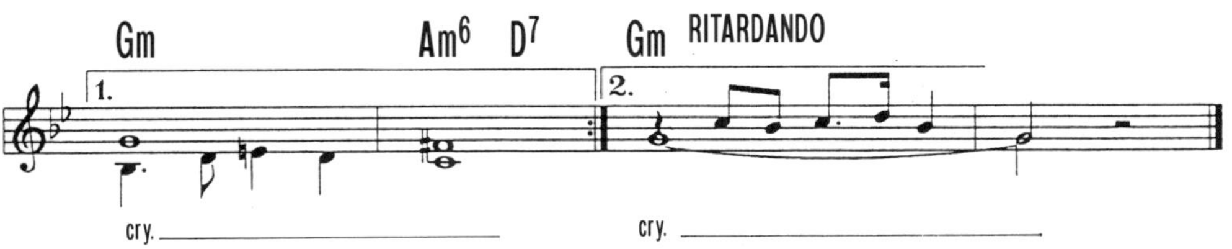

2. One of these mornin's, you goin' to rise up singin'
Then you'll spread yo' wings an' you'll take the sky.
But till that mornin, there's a nothin' can harm you
With Daddy an' Mammy standin' by

SWANEE River

Traditional
Interpret: Bing Crosby
Rhythmus: Medium Song
Tempo: Moderato

2. All round the little farm I wandered when I was young;
The many happy days I squandered, many the songs I sung.
When I was playing with my brother happy was I.
Oh! Take me to my kind old mother, there let me live and die! ...

3. One little hut among the bushes, one that I love,
Still sadly to my mem'ry rushes no matter where I rove.
When will I see the bees a humming, all round the comb?
When will I hear the banjo tumming down in my good old home ...

Take On Me

Musik: Paul Waaktarr/ Mags
Text: Morten Harket/ Pal Waaktarr/ Mags
Interpreten: AHA
Rhythmus: Rock
Tempo: Medium

© by ATV Music Ltd.,
MCA Music GmbH, Hamburg für Deutschland,
Österreich, Schweiz und Ostblock

2. So, needless to say at odds and ends
But I'll be stumbling away
Slowly learning that life is O.K.
Say after me
It's much better to be safe than sorry.

3. Oh, things that you say
Yeah, is it life or just a play my worries away
You're all the things I've got to remember
You shine away
I'll be coming for you anyway.

The Girl from IPANEMA

Originaltext: Vinicius De Moraes
Engl. Text: Norman Gimbel
Musik: Antonio Carlos Jobim
Rhythmus: Bossa Nova
Tempo: Moderato

© 1963, 1970, 1979 by
Antonio Carlos Jobim & Vinicius De Moraes.
MCA Music GmbH Hamburg,
für D, A, CH und Ostblock

F#m7 D7
can I tell her I love her? Yes
Gm7 Eb7
I would give my heart glad – ly. But each
Am7 D9b Gm7 C9b
day when she walks to the sea, she looks straight a – head not at me.
Fmaj7 G7
Tall and tan and young and love – ly, the girl from I – pa-ne – ma goes walk – ing and when
Gm7 Gb7 Fmaj7
she pas-ses I smile, but she does-n't see.

the House of the rising sun

Traditional
Interpreten: Eric Burdon and the Animals
Rhythmus: Ballade
Tempo: Slow

2. My mother is a taylor,
She sewed my new blue jeans,
My sweetheart is a drunkard Lord,
Down in New Orleans.

3. Well, the only thing a drunkard needs
Is a suitcase and a trunk
And the only time he's satisfied
Is when he's on a drunk.

The Sloop John B.

Traditional
Interpretiert von den Beach Boys
Rhythmus: West Coast Rock
Tempo: ♩=114

2. The first mate he got drunk,
Break up the people's trunk,
Constable come aboard and take him away,
Mr. Johnstone, please let me alone,
I feel so break up, I want to go home!
So, hoist up the John B. ...

3. The poor cook he got fits,
Throw 'way all the grits,
Then he took and eat up all o' my corn,
Let me go home, I want to go home!
This is the worst trip since I been born!
So, hoist up the John B. ...

TIME after TIME

Text und Musik:
Lauper/ Hyman
Interpreten: Cindy Lauper, Miles Davis
Rhythmus: Rock
Tempo: Moderato

© by Rella Music,
Sony Music Publishing
für D, A, CH und Osteuropa

F G Em F G Em
you say go slow. I fall be – hind.
Sec – rets sto – len from deep in – side
F G Em F G Am
The sec – ond hand un – winds. If you're lost you can look and you will find me
The drum beats out of time.
F G C G Am
time af – ter time. If you fall I will catch you, I'll be wait – ing
F G C G Am
time af – ter time. If you're lost you can look and you will find me
F G C G Am
time af – ter time. If you fall I will catch you, I'll be wait – ing
F G C F
1.
time af – ter time.
G Em F C D.S.
2.
F G C F G C FADE OUT
time af – ter time, time af – ter time.

TO LOVE SOMEBODY

Musik und Text:
Barry Gibb/ Robin Gibb
Interpreten: Bee Gees, Jimmy Somerville
Rhythmus: Rock Ballade oder Reggae
Tempo: Moderato

© by Gibb Bros. Music
Musik-Edition Discoton GmbH
(BMG UFA Musikverlage), München
für D, A, CH und Ostblock

2. In my brain I see your face again; I know my face of mind.
You ain't not to be so blind, so very blind.
I'm a man, can't you see what I am? I live and I breathe for you.
But what good does it do, if I ain't got you, ain't got you?

TOM DOOLEY

Traditional
Interpreten: Kingston Trio
Rhythmus: Ballade
Tempo: ♩ =108

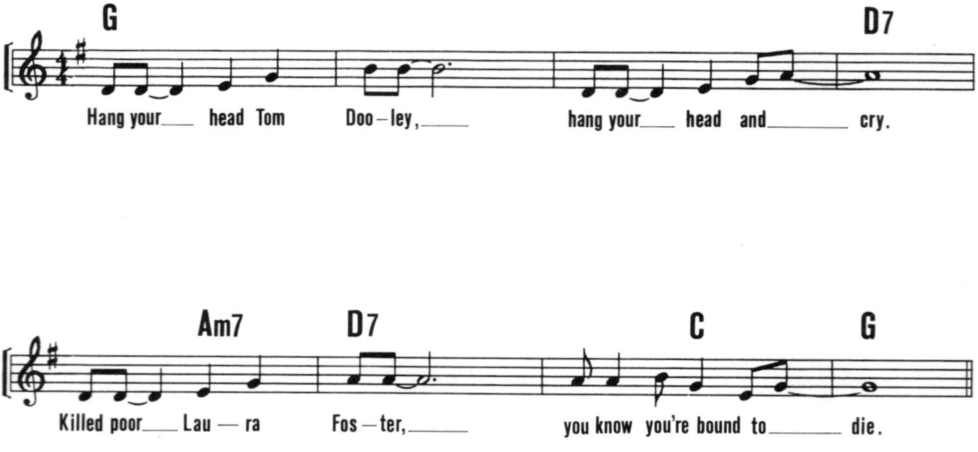

2. You took her on the hillside
As god almighty knows,
You took her on the hillside,
And there you hid her clothes.

3. You took her on the hillside
To make her your wife,
You took her on the hillside,
Where there you took her life.

4. Take down my old violin
And play it all you please,
At this time tomorrow
It'll be no use to me.

5. I dug a grave four feet long,
I dug it three feet deep,
And throw'd the cold clay o'er her
And tramped it with my feet.

6. This world and one more then
Where do you reckon I'd be?
If it hadn't been for Grayson
I'd-a-been in Tennessee.

TONIGHT

Musik und Text:
David Bowie/ Iggy Pop
Interpretiert von David Bowie und Tina Turner
Rhythmus: Reggae
Tempo: ♩=98

© by Bewlay Brothers Music/
Fleur Music/ Osterberg Music.
Für D, A, CH und osteuropäische Länder:
EMI Music Publishing Germany GmbH, Hamburg/
Virgin Music Publishers Germany

A E
to - night.
A E F♯m F♯m^SUS4 F♯m
I will love you 'til I reach the end.
A E F♯m F♯m^SUS4 F♯m
I will love you 'til I reach the end.
D A E D
I will love you 'til I die I will see you in the sky to-night
A E
to night
E D A
to night to night.

Tutti Frutti

Text und Musik:
Richard Penniman/ Dorothy La Bostrie
Interpreten: Little Richard, Elvis Presley
Rhythmus: Rock'n Roll
Tempo: Allegro

© 1955 by Venice Music Inc. c/o ATV Music Group,
MCA Music GmbH, Hamburg für D, A, CH und Ostblock

F F7
gal, name's Sue. She knows just what to do. I got a
gal, name's Daisy. She al – ways drives me cra – zy. I got a
B♭7 F
gal, name's Sue. She knows just what to do. She
gal, name's Daisy. She al – ways drives me cra – zy. She
F
rock to the east, she rock to the west, but she's the gal that I love best. Tut-ti
knows how to love me, yes, in-deed. Boy, you don't know what she do to me.
frut-ti au-rut – ti, tut-ti frut – ti au – rut – ti. Ooh, tut – ti
B♭7 F
frut – ti au – rut – ti, tut – ti frut-ti au – rut – ti, tut-ti
C7 F
1. 2. D.S.
frut-ti au-rut – ti, a – wop-bop-a-loom-op a – lop-bomp-bom! I got a ow! Tutti lop-bam-boom.

Wade in the water

Traditional
Interpret: Alexis Korner
Rhythmus: Medium Rock
Tempo: Moderato

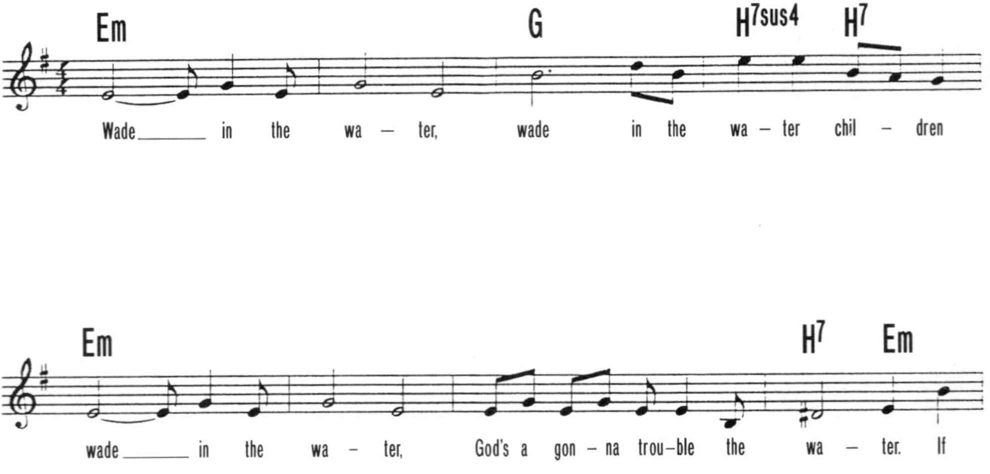

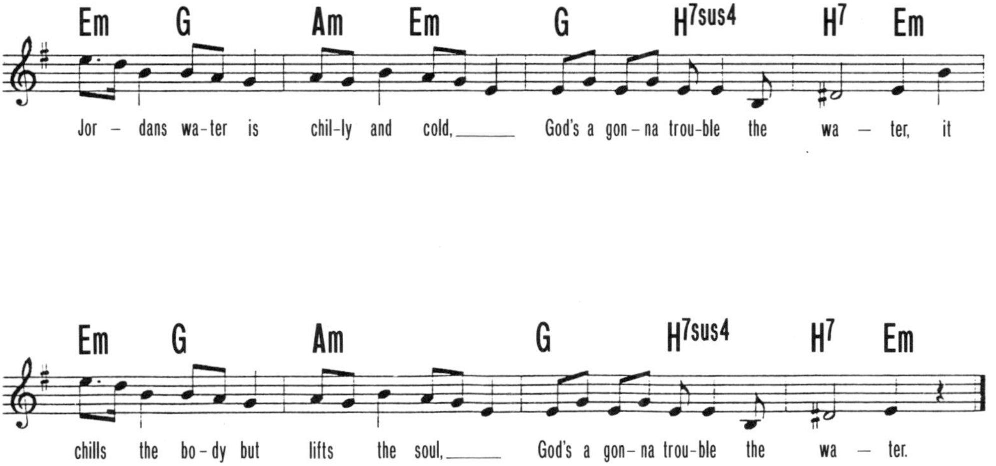

2. See that band all dressed in red,
God's gonna trouble these waters,
Look like a band that Moses led,
God's gonna trouble these waters.
Wade in the water, wade in the water, children,
Wade in the water, God's a gonna trouble the water.

Waiting for a girl like YOU

Text und Musik: Lou Gramm/ Mick Jones
Interpret: Foreigner
Rhythmus: Rock Ballade
Tempo: Moderato

© by Somerset Songs Publ. Inc., USA,
Intersong USA Inc.
Für Deutschland: Musikverlag Intersong GmbH, Hamburg

2. You're so good. When we make love it's understood.
It's more than a touch or a word we say. Only in dreams could it be this way.
When you love someone, yeah, really love someone,
It feels so right, so warm and true. I need to know if you feel it too.
Now I know it's right from the moment I wake up till deep in the night.
There's nowhere on earth that I'd rather be than holding you tenderly.
I've been waiting for a girl like you, a love that will survive.
I've been waiting for someone new to make me feel alive.
Yeah, waiting for a girl like you to come into my life.

Was wird morgen sein

Musik: Dietrich Kessler
Text: Jan Witte
Rhythmus: Rock Ballade
Tempo: Slow

© by KDM Records & Verlag
1000 Berlin 30

Em Am H Em
Sag, was wird mor– gen sein, bau'n wir nur auf Sand, bau'n wir uns in Stein?
Em Am H Em Em Am Em Am
Sag' was wird morgen sein, gehn wir Hand in Hand o – der ganzal – lein?
Em Am D G H7
Werden wir noch alt, so wie's uns gefällt, oder lebst Du bald in ei–ner and'ren Welt?
Em Am D G H7 Em
D.S.
Tausend Fragen frage ich Dich heut' nicht mehr, alles was ich sag' Du, ich lieb Dich sehr. lein?

We can work it out

Text und Musik: John Lennon/ Paul McCartney
Interpret: Beatles
Rhythmus: Medium Rock
Tempo: Allegro

© by Northern Songs Ltd.,
MCA Music GmbH, Hamburg für Deutschland,
Österreich, Schweiz und Ostblock

2. Think of what you're saying, you can get it wrong and still you think that it's alright.
Think of what I'm saying, we can work it out and get it straight or say good night.

WE WILL ROCK YOU

Musik und Text:
Brian May
Interpreten: Queen
Rhythmus: Rock
Tempo: Moderato

© by Queen Music Ltd., London.
Rechte für D, A, CH, osteuropäische Länder:
EMI Music Publishing Germany GmbH, Hamburg

2. Buddy you're a young man, hard man shoutin' in the street
Gonna take on the world some day,
You got blood on yo' face, you big disgrace
Wavin' your banner all over the place, Singin' ...

3. Buddy you're an old man, poor man pleadin' with your eyes
Gonna make you some peace some day
You got mud on your face, you big disgrace,
Somebody better put your back into your place, singin' ...

When the Saints go marching in

Traditional
Interpreten: Louis Armstrong, Bill Haley
Rhythmus: Swing
Tempo: ♩ =138

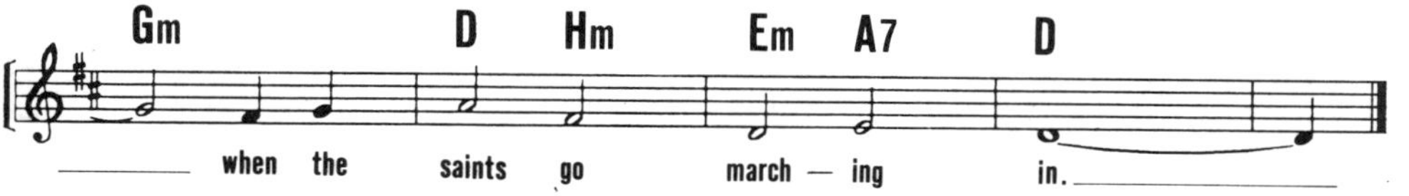

2. And when the revelation comes,
And when the revelation comes,
Oh, Lord, I want to be in that number,
When the revelation comes.

3. Oh, when the new world is revealed,
Oh, when the new world is revealed,
Oh, Lord, I want to be in that number,
When the new world is revealed.

4. Oh, when they gather 'round the throne,
Oh, when they gather 'round the throne,
Oh, Lord, I want to be in that number,
When they gather 'round the throne.

5. And when they crown him King of Kings,
And when they crown him King of Kings,
Oh, Lord, I want to be in that number,
When they crown him King of Kings.

6. And when the sun no more will shine,
And when the sun no more will shine,
Oh, Lord, I want to be in that number,
When the sun no more will shine.

7. And when the moon has turned to blood,
And when the moon has turned to blood,
Oh, Lord, I want to be in that number,
When the moon has turned to blood.

8. And when the earth has turned to fire,
And when the earth has turned to fire,
Oh, Lord, I want to be in that number,
When the earth has turned to fire.

9. And on that Hallelujah Day,
And on that Hallelujah Day,
Oh, Lord I want to be in that number,
On that Hallelujah Day.

10. Oh, when the Saints go marching in,
Oh, when the Saints go marching in,
Oh, Lord, I want to be in that number,
When the Saints go marching in.

WITH A LITTLE HELP FROM MY FRIENDS

Musik und Text:
John Lennon/ Paul McCartney
Interpreten: Beatles/ Joe Cocker
Rhythmus: Swing Feeling
Tempo: Moderato

© by Northern Songs Ltd.,
MCA Music GmbH, Hamburg für Deutschland,
Österreich, Schweiz und Ostblock

2. What do I do when my love is away,
Does it worry you to be alone?
How do I feel by the end of the day,
Are you sad becuase you're on your own? No, I get by...

3. Would you believe in a love at first sight?
Yes, I'm certain that it happens all the time.
What do you see when you turn out the light?
I can't tell you, but I know it's mine. Oh, I get by...

Yesterday

Musik und Text:
John Lennon/ Paul McCartney
Interpreten: Beatles
Rhythmus: Rock Ballade
Tempo: Moderato

© by Northern Songs Ltd.,
MCA Music GmbH, Hamburg für Deutschland,
Österreich, Schweiz und Ostblock

2. Suddenly, I'm not half the man I used to be,
There's a shadow hangin' over me,
Oh, yesterday came suddenly.

you are the Sunshine of my life

Musik und Text:
Stevie Wonder
Interpret: Stevie Wonder
Rhythmus: Medium Swing
Tempo: Moderato

© 1972 by Jobete/ Black Bull Music Inc., USA.
Rechte für D, A, CH, osteuropäische Länder:
EMI Music Publishing Germany GmbH, Hamburg

2. You must have known that I was lonely,
Because you came to my rescue.
And I know that this must be heaven;
How could so much love be inside of you.

Senza una Donna
(Without A Woman)

Musik und Originaltext:
Adelmo Fornaciari
Englischer Text: T. Musker
Interpreten: Zucchero/ Paul Young
Rhythmus: Rock Ballade
Tempo: Moderato

© 1987 by Warner Chappell Music Italiana.
Für Deutschland, Österreich und osteuropäische Länder:
Hanseatic Musikverlag GmbH, Hamburg

D A Hm A D A G A
donna, no more pain and no sorrow, senza una donna I'll make it through tomorrow, senza una
D A Hm A D A G A F#7
1.
donna given me tor-tue and bliss. Without a woman better like this.
Hm G D A F#7 Hm A
2.
3.
tor-tue and bliss ooh tor-tue and bliss. Without a
G D A D A
wo-man, vie-ni qui! Come on in senza una don-na I don't
Hm A D A G A
know what might follow, senza una donna, oh, may be from to-morrow senza una
D A Hm A G A D
3
donna, given me tor-tue and bliss, ooh

WIND of CHANGE

Musik und Text:
Klaus Meine
Interpreten: Scorpions
Rhythmus: Rock Ballade
Tempo: Slow

© 1990 by PRI Music Inc.
Für D, A, CH: Polygram Songs Musikverlag GmbH

C Dm C Dm Am7 G5
I follow the Mos – kwa, down to Gor-ki Park, listening to the wind of change.
C G5 Dm G5 C G5
Take me to the ma-gic of a mo–ment on a glo – ry night, when the
Dm G5 Am Am/F G5 Am
childrenof tomorrow share their dreams with you and me. The wind of change blows
dream a – way in the wind of change.
G5 Am G5
straight in – to the face of time, like a stormwind that will ring the freedom – bell for peace of
C Dm E
mind. Let your Bala – laika sing what my guitar wants to say.
C G5 Dm G5 C G5
Take me to the ma – gic of a mo-ment on a glo – ry night, where the
Dm G5 Am Am/F G5 G5
children of to – morrow share their dreams with you and me.
dream a – way in the wind of change.
(Pfeifen 8va) F Dm F
Dm Am7 Dm

Dur Moll Dur7 Moll7

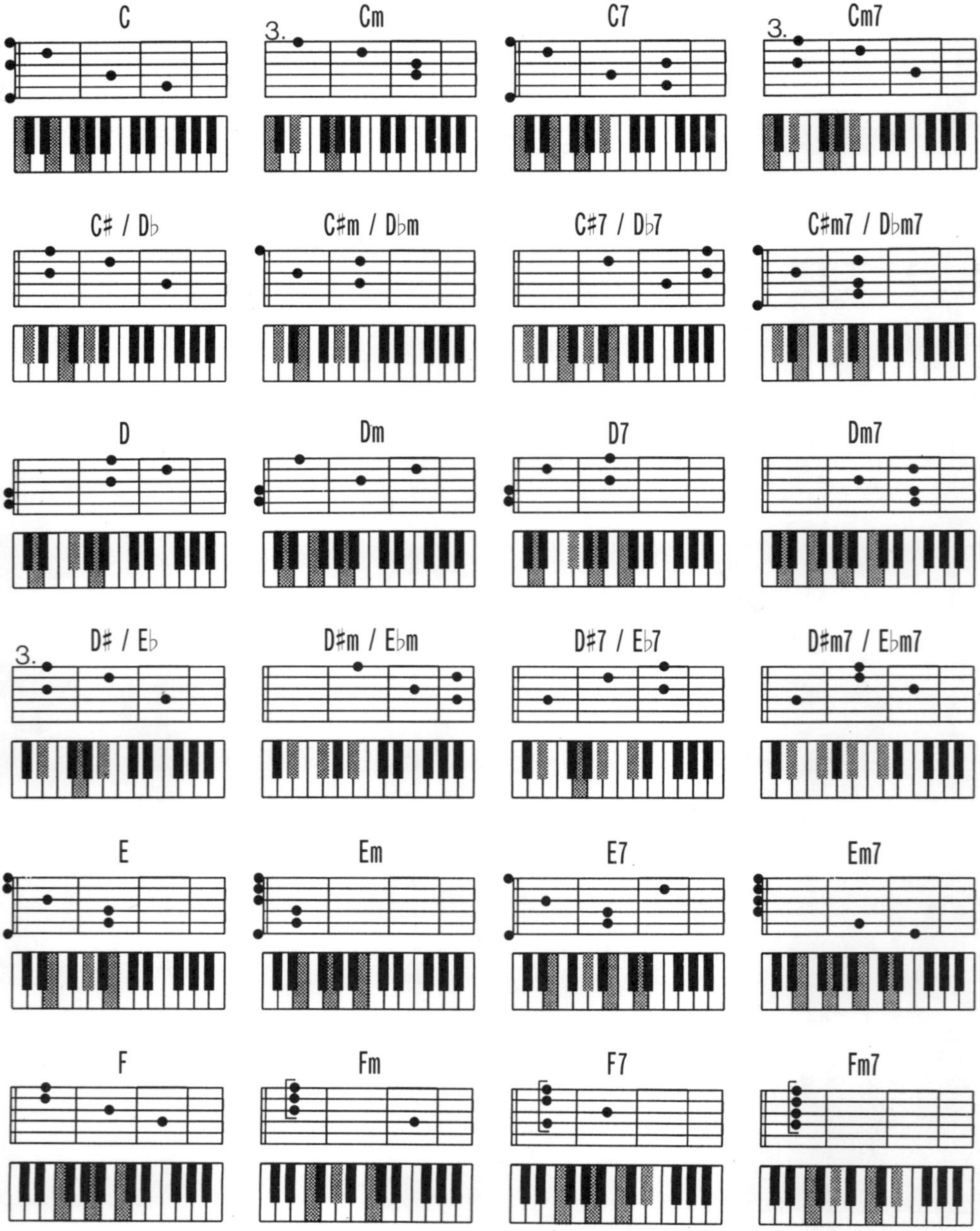

Dur	Moll	Dur7	Moll7

F# / G♭

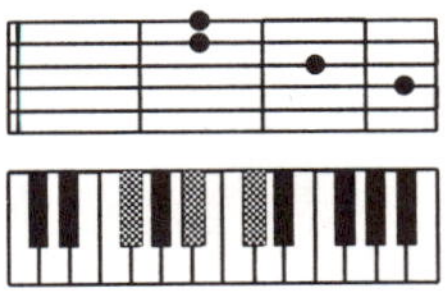

F#m / G♭m

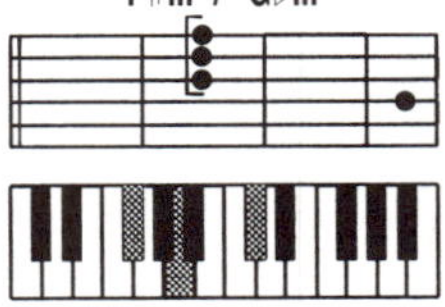

F#7 / G♭7

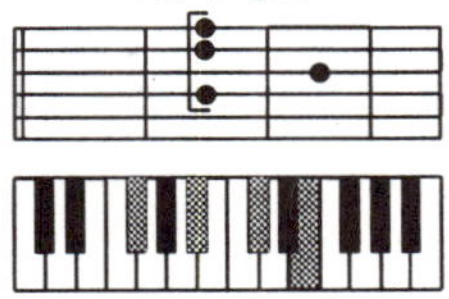

F#m7 / G♭m7

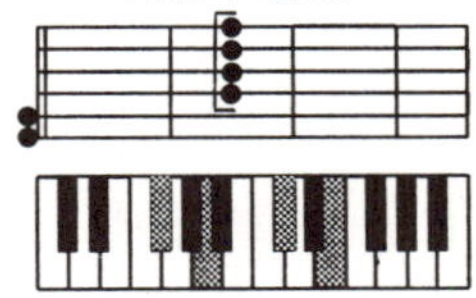

G

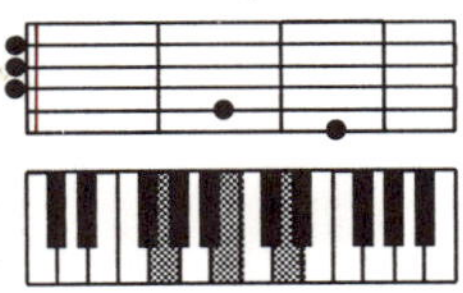

Gm

3.

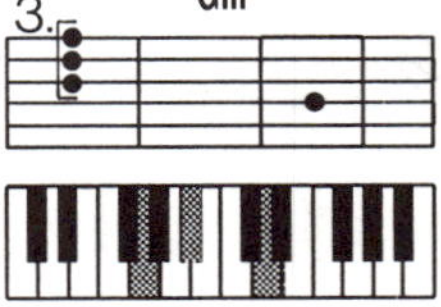

G7

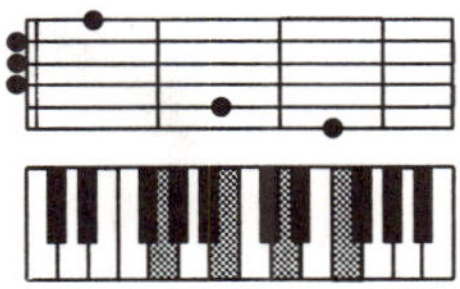

Gm7

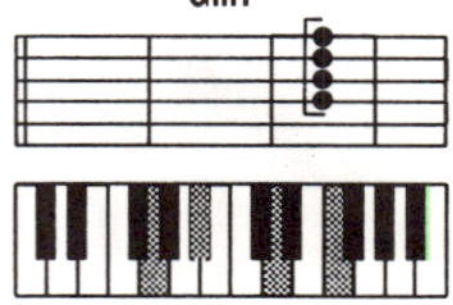

G# / A♭

3.

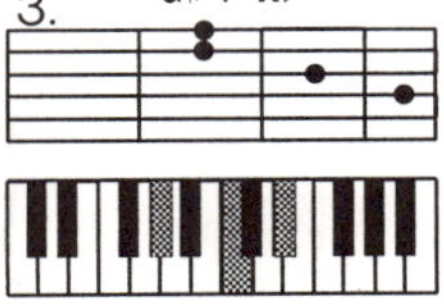

G#m / A♭m

3.

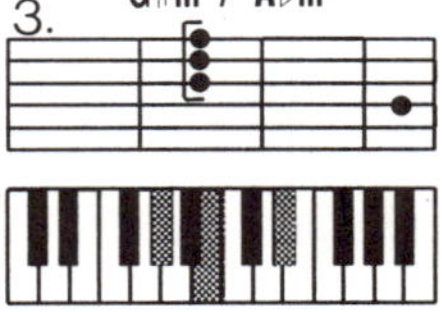

G#7 / A♭7

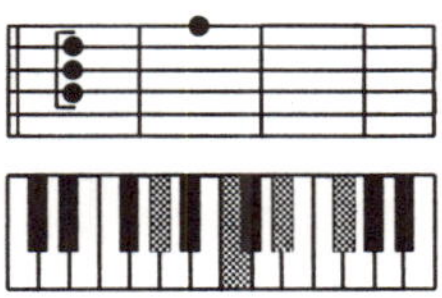

G#m7 / A♭m7

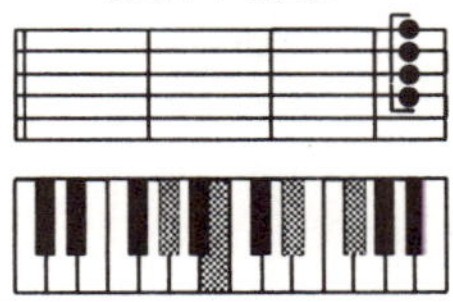

A

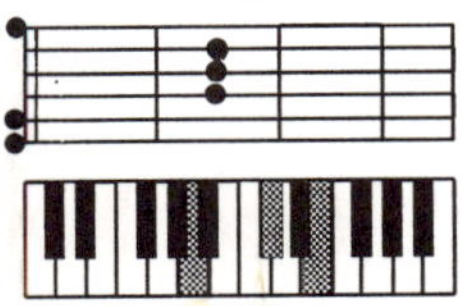

Am

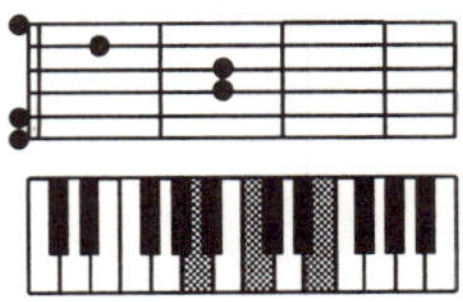

A7

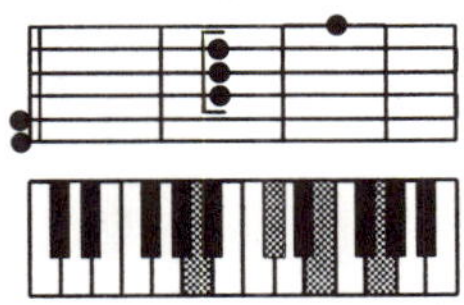

Am7

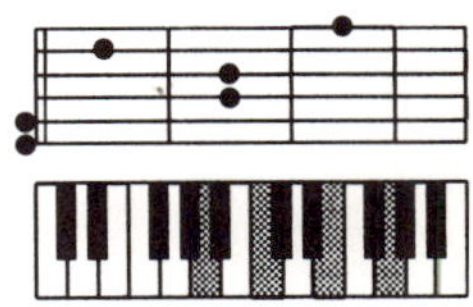

A# / B♭

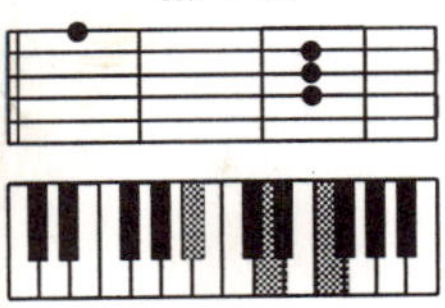

A#m / B♭m

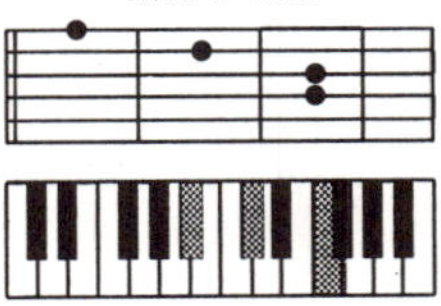

A#7 / B♭7

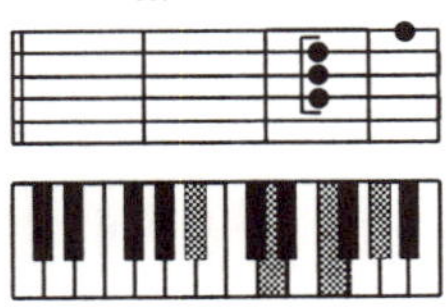

A#m7 / B♭m7

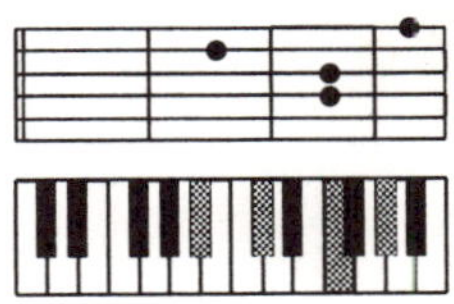

H

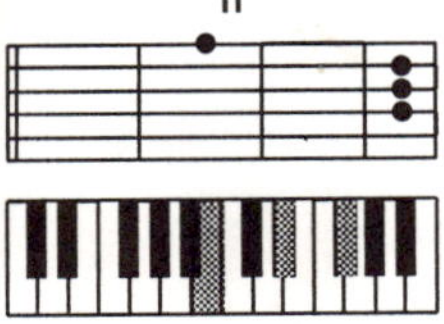

Hm

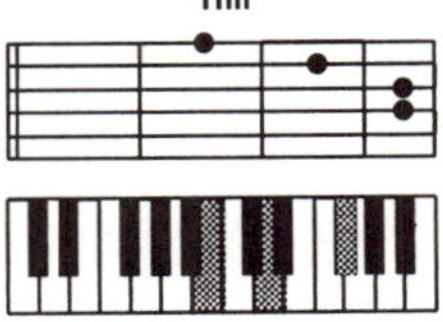

H7

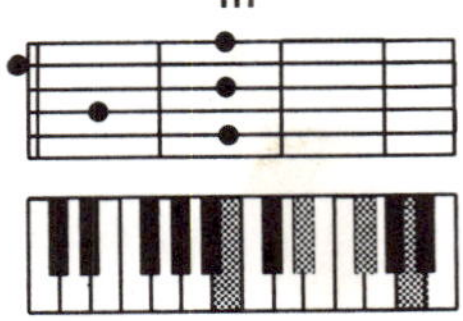

Hm7

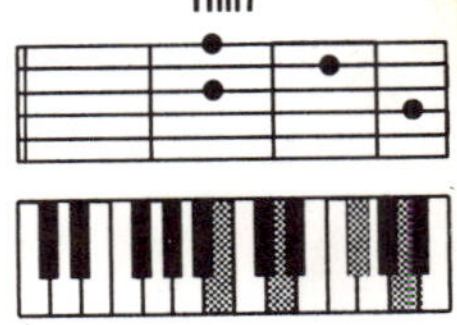

Dur^{maj7} Dur^{sus4} O +

Cj7

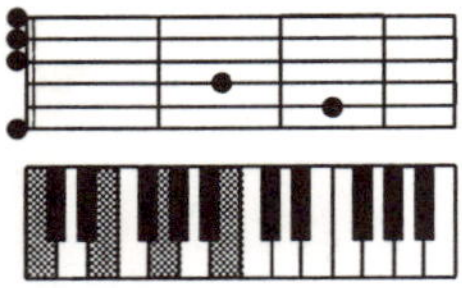

Csus4

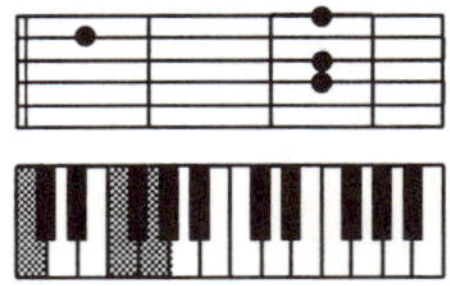

C°

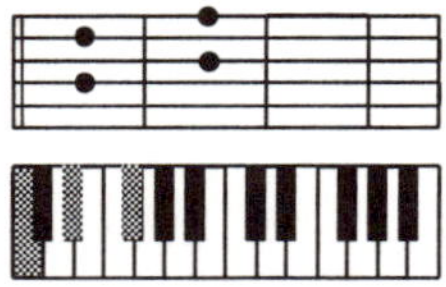

C+

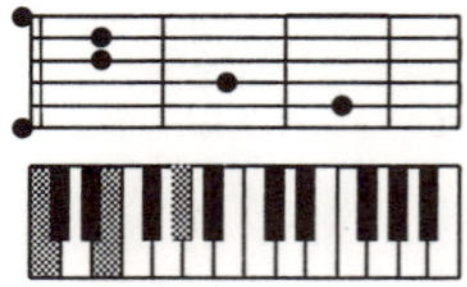

C♯j7 / D♭j7

C♯sus4 / D♭sus4

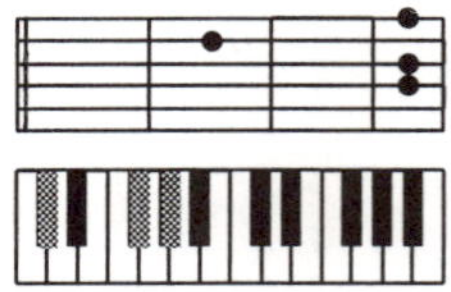

C♯° / D♭°

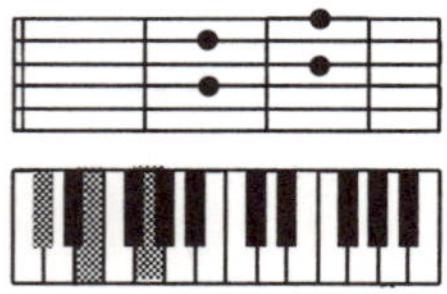

C♯+ / D♭+

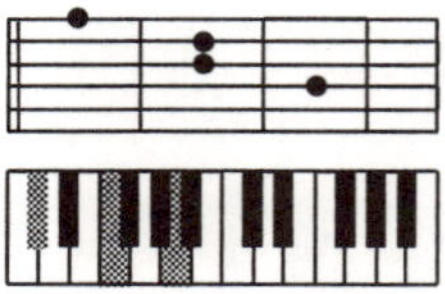

Dj7

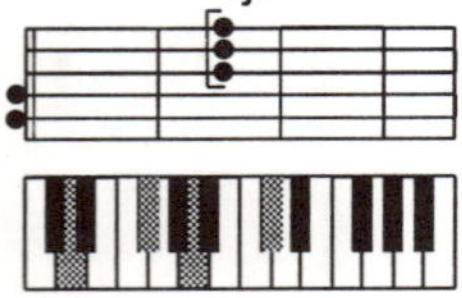

Dsus4

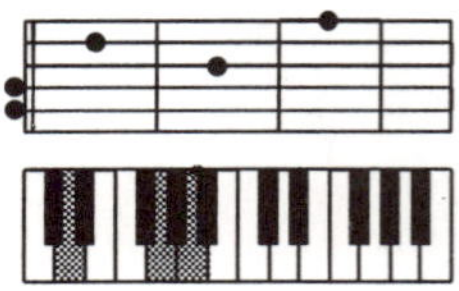

D°

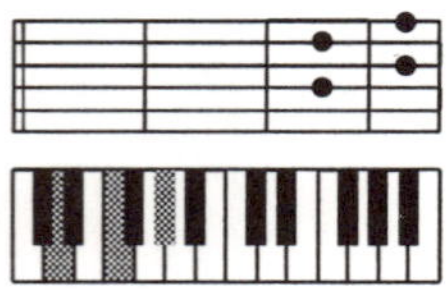

D+

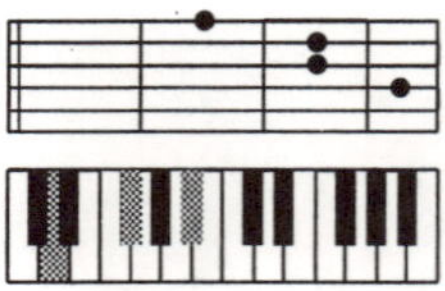

D♯j7 / E♭j7

D♯sus4 / E♭sus4

D♯° / E♭°

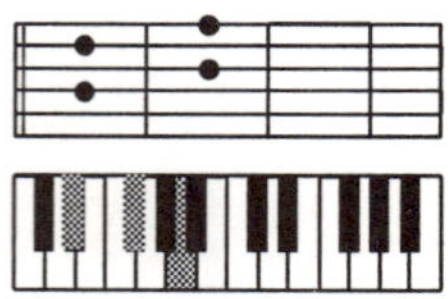

D♯+ / E♭+

Ej7

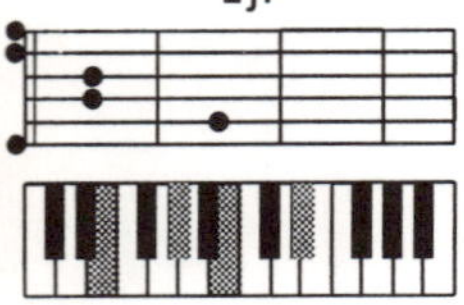

Esus4

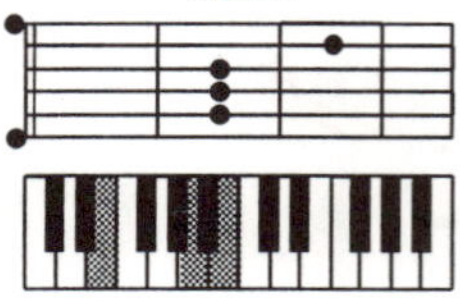

E°

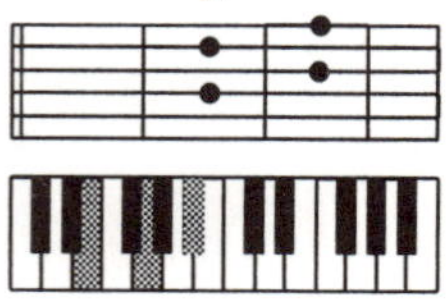

E+

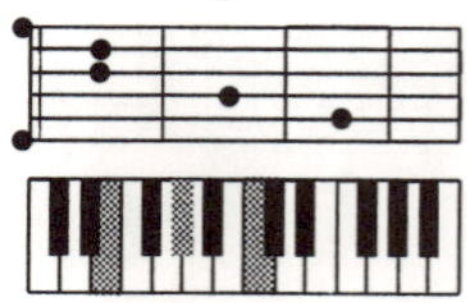

Fj7

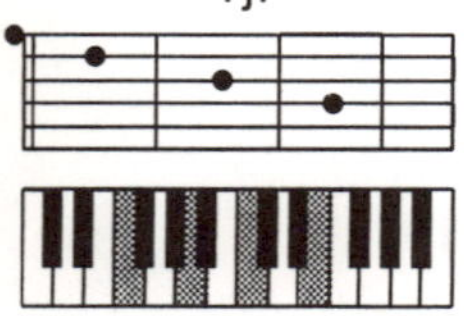

Fsus4

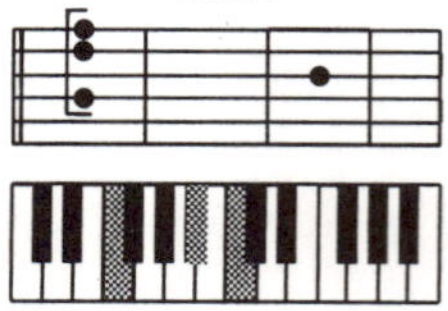

F°

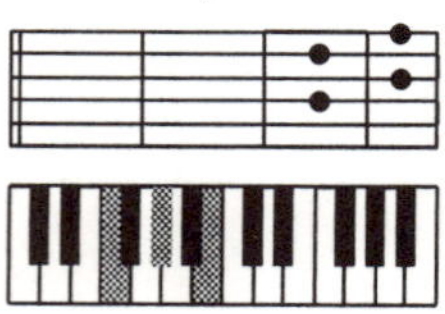

F+

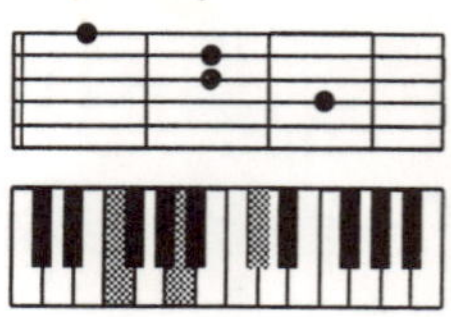

Dur^{maj7}

F♯j7 / G♭j7

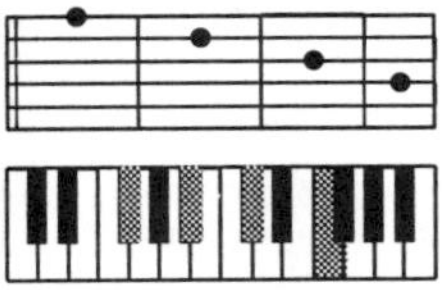

Gj7

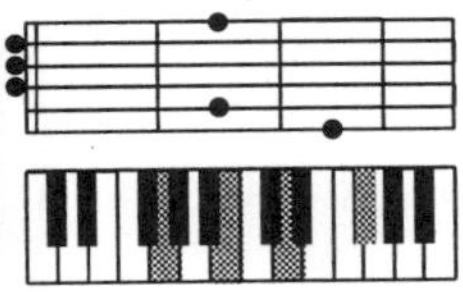

G♯j7 / A♭j7

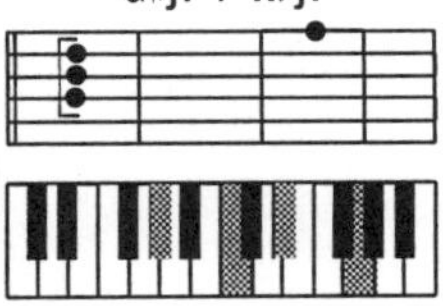

Aj7

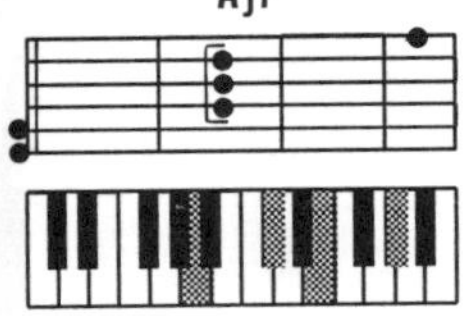

A♯j7 / B♭j7

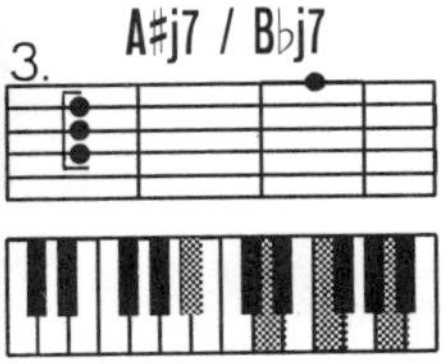

Hj7

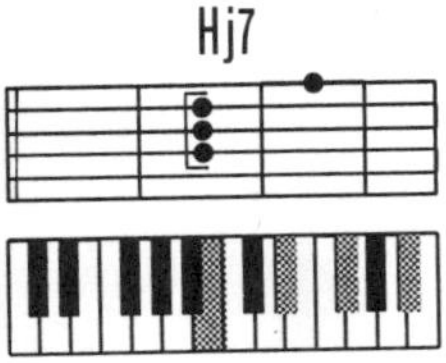

Dur^{sus4}

F♯sus4 / G♭sus4

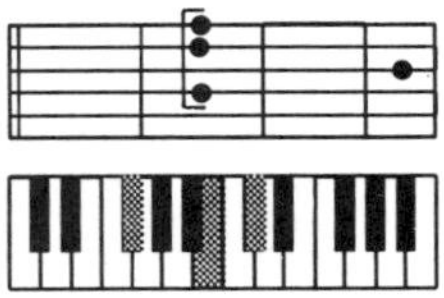

Gsus4

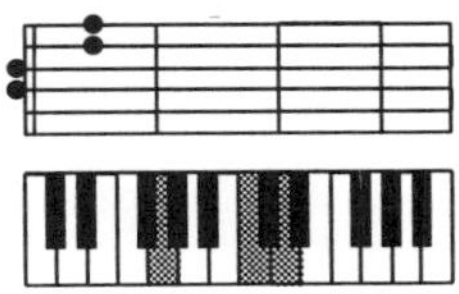

G♯sus4 / A♭sus4

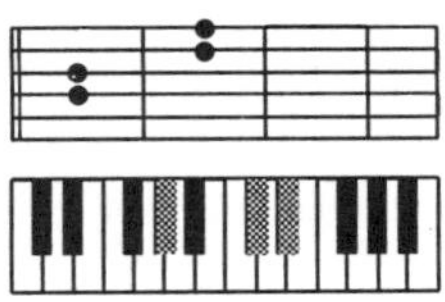

Asus4

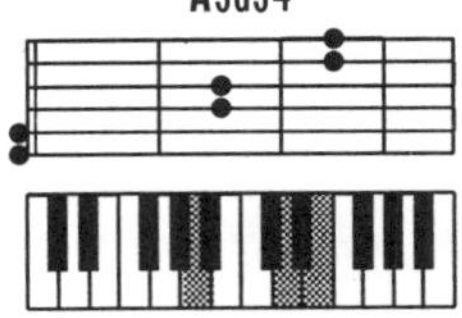

A♯sus4 / B♭sus4

Hsus4

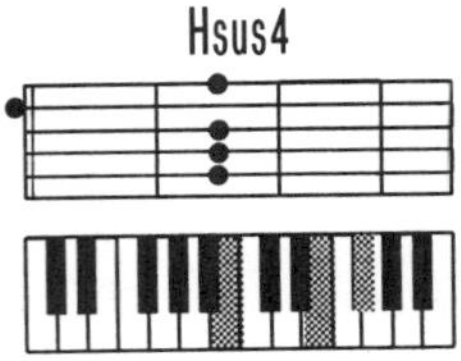

o

F♯° / G♭°

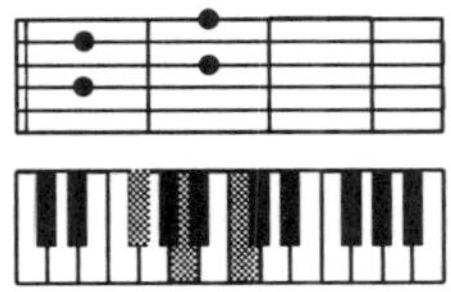

G°

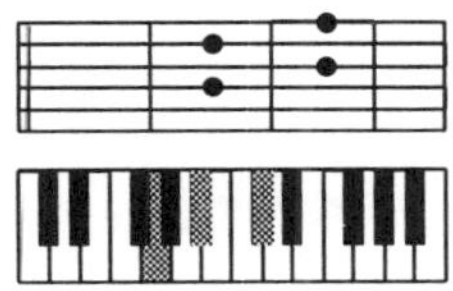

G♯° / A♭°

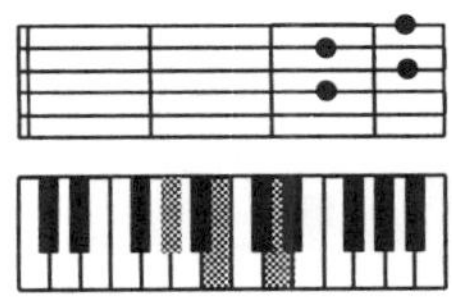

A°

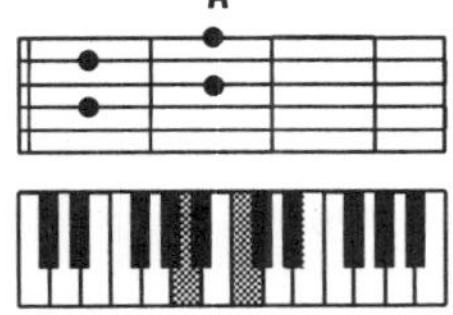

A♯° / B♭°

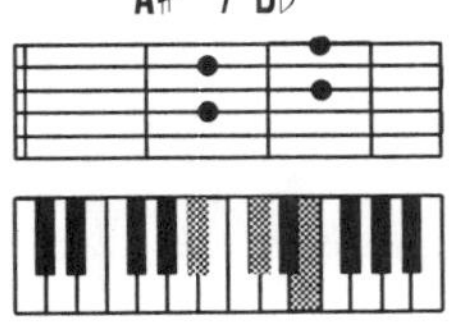

H°

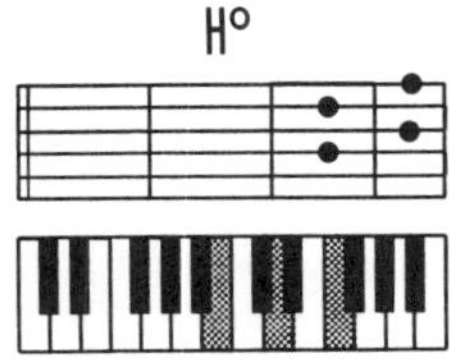

+

F♯+ / G♭+

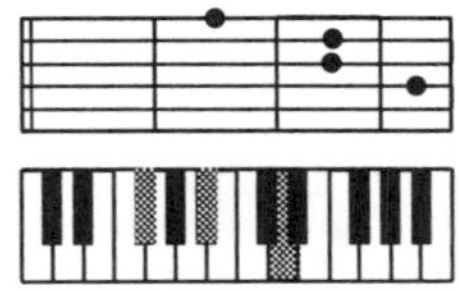

G+

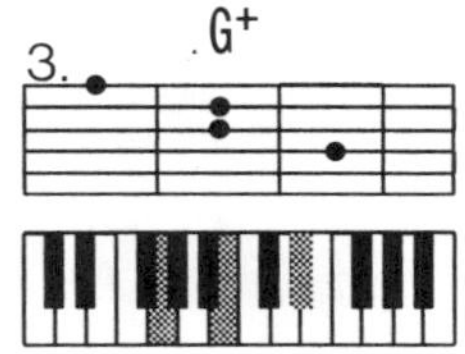

G♯+ / A♭+

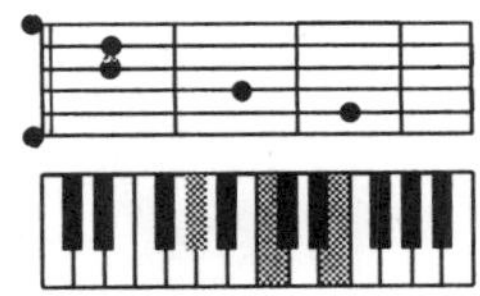

A+

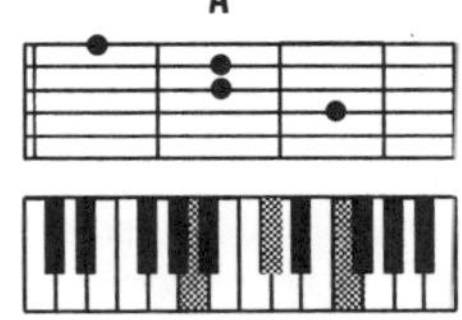

A♯+ / B♭+

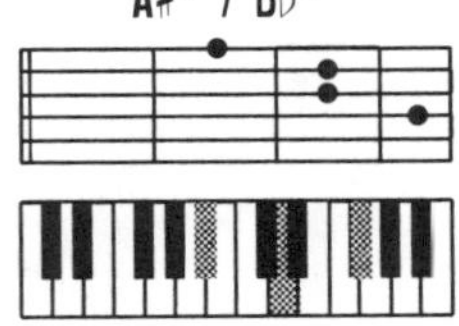

H+

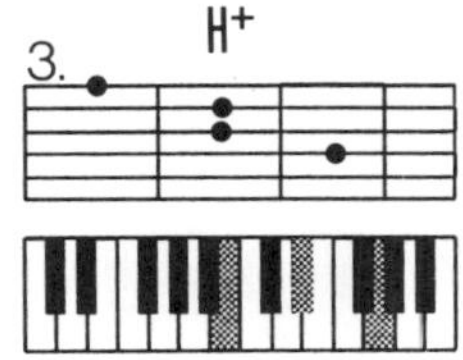

Qualität aus Berlin!

KDM PRÄSENTIERT:

VERLAG

Die Standardwerke
für anspruchsvolle Gitarristen

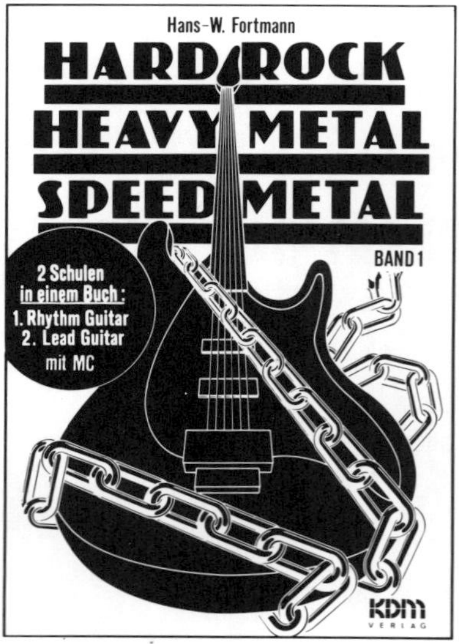

Band 1, 2 und 3

Diese neue Keyboardschule
erscheint in mehreren Bänden

Das neue Buch
für den kreativen Keyboarder

Band 1 und 2

Eine neue und
moderne Musiklehre